Discovering the Future:
The Business of Paradigms

By Joel Arthur Barker

ILI Press
St. Paul, MN

Dedication

To Mom and Dad, to Susan and Kelly, and especially to my son, Andrew, who has taught me more about life than any other person...May all of your futures be peaceful ones.

Acknowledgments

As in any endeavor, it takes more than one person to be successful. I would like to thank the following people for their help and influence on this book:

David Lilly who provided, in 1973, the funds for the fellowship that gave me my start in futures studies;

T. Lance Holthusen who hired me as education specialist for the Future Studies Department of the Science Museum of Minnesota;

Bill Weimer who provided key opportunities to share my thoughts on paradigms with a number of critical yet appreciative business groups;

Scott Erickson, my partner and fellow futurist, who helped me think more carefully about the ideas in this book;

Bobbi Berwin who typed the initial manuscripts;

Diana Smith who finished the project and spent hundreds of hours with me on the fine tuning of the book;

Elaine Erickson who proofread the book and offered additional comments for improvement;

Susan Whitney Barker, my partner and wife, who put up with my frustrations and delays and provided unflagging support.

To all of you, thanks. I hope you are as pleased with this book as I am.

JAB

Contents

Foreword

1   The Importance of Anticipation   1
    List of fundamental changes
    Anticipation in turbulent times
    Manager's Skills Domain
    Components of Strategic Exploration

2   Paradigms   12
    Definitions
    Author's definition
    Trend-Paradigm relationship

3   The Setting for the Shift   17
    Thomas Kuhn's Importance
    Breadth of the idea
    The four questions
    Paradigm-evolution curve
    Unsolved problems as triggers

4   Enter the "Shifter"   25
    First two kinds
    The tinkerer
    Classic responses
    New paradigms and risk

5   The Paradigm Pioneers   34
    What drives them to change
    Act of faith
    Rewards for the pioneer

6   The Paradigm Effect   40
    Kuhn's observations
    Broadening the impact

7   Nine Examples   46

8   Key Characteristics of Paradigms   67
Functional importance
More than one right answer
Paradigm paralysis
Paradigm pliancy
The paradigm shift question

9   The Evolution of Paradigms   78
Problem-solving efficiency
Cost-per-problem solved
Paradigm bridging

10   Going Back to Zero   90
Definition of the rule
IBM and Apple

11   Looking Forward   97
The testing question
Nurse administrators answers
Write your own list
Some emerging paradigms

12   And So It Goes   119
Experts' errors
Arthur C. Clarke's observations
Steps needed for radical change to occur

The Last Chapter   129
Inventorying your own paradigm
Reading to stretch – some recommendations
Periodicals to read
The Pig and the Sow – a parable

Additional Paradigm Tools   140
Additional books
Discovering the Future – the film
Profiting from Paradigms – an audiotape series

Foreword

I have been a futurist officially for fourteen years, uno-
fficially for all but the first six years of my life. In 1972,
I received a one-year grant that allowed me to travel
around the United States and, ultimately, to Europe.
My principal purpose was to discover what kinds of
future-related materials and techniques were being
taught to kindergarten through twelfth-grade students. I planned to use this information to help create
a futures-studies curriculum at St. Paul Academy and
Summit School in St. Paul, Minnesota, where I was
teaching at the time.

As a result of that experience, my life changed dramatically. I left the Academy the next year and joined
the Science Museum of Minnesota, where T. Lance
Holthusen had created a futures-studies department in
a science museum—the first of its kind in the Western
Hemisphere. The next year, I became director of that

department which, through a series of programs and exhibits over the next four years, helped Minnesotans explore an array of possible futures awaiting them.

In 1978, I left the Science Museum to form my own company, Infinity Limited, Inc. Since then, I have worked with many organizations, including major world corporations, nonprofit institutions, small entrepreneurial businesses, educational institutions, churches, and professional groups.

While I have spoken on the long-term implications of many issues, one topic in particular has been enormously popular since the first time I spoke about it in 1974. It is, even today, my most requested lecture. I have presented it to students, to business leaders, to government staff, to church officials. And, almost always, those presentations result in more presentations.

In this speech, I have identified and clarified a key concept concerning the future which helps my audiences understand many of the events of the last twenty years and gives them a much better perspective of what may happen over the next twenty years. After each speech, someone inevitably asks me, "Do you have a book on this?" Until now, my response has been, "I'm working on it."

Actually, when I outlined the book the first time, it was much longer. But the more I worked on the outline, the more I realized that I had not one but three books. This is the first of those three: it will focus on the key concept—"the business of paradigms."

I know that the concepts in this book have helped many people deal with our turbulent world more effectively because they have told me so. So, I invite you to join me in a four-hour exploration on how to discover the future.

One final comment. I would like to thank all of those people who, over the years, have continued to both encourage and pester me about this book. It was always easier to give a speech than to write it down, and I probably wouldn't have written this without their persistence.

1   The Importance of Anticipation

The field of futures studies became public when Alvin Toffler published his now classic *Future Shock* in 1970. This book demonstrated to a wide audience the importance of trying to anticipate the future, to understand the potential implications – positive and negative – before they occurred.

Futures studies or futurism or futurology (I don't like that label at all), however, had already had a substantial although secluded life long before Alvin Toffler appeared on the scene. During World War II in the military and then after the war in the work of the Rand Corporation, Standford Research Institute (now SRI International), Ted Gordon's Futures Group, and the Hudson Institute, the concept of studying the future in a serious and rigorous way grew throughout the '50s and '60s.

But it took the chaos and resulting turbulence of the

'70s to bring this field of study out of the scholarly closet and into the living room of public visibility. These days you expect to read articles about the future in magazines, find books about the future in the bookstore, watch TV shows whose primary purpose is to give you information about possible futures ahead. The study of the future is a piece of the conceptual landscape because we, as members of a global society, have come to value the skills of anticipation.

The field of future studies can be broken up into two general areas: content futurism and process futurism. A content futurist is a person who specializes in an area of information about the future. Whether it is robotics or telecommunications, energy or water usage, shelter design or nutrition, content futurists speculate on the "whats" of the future. Process futurism, the area I have chosen to focus on, deals with **how to think** about the "what." In my own work, I have often found that people have significant amounts of content about possible futures but have no way of making that information useful. Process futurists teach them how to manipulate that information.

I want to teach you about a concept that can help you to discover the future with greater accuracy. It is a way of fishing for the future.

In the last twenty years, all of Western society has been through extraordinarily turbulent times. We have been living in a time when fundamental rules, the basic ways we do things, have been altered dramatically. That is, what was right and appropriate in the early '60s is now, in many cases, wrong and highly inappropriate in the '80s. Or, conversely, what was impossible, crazy, or clearly out of line in the early '60s, is, in many cases today, so ordinary that we forget that it wasn't always that way. These kinds of dramatic changes are extremely important because they have created in us a special sense of impermanence which generates tremendous discomfort.

Let's take a look at an abbreviated list of those kinds of fundamental changes:

- The introduction of environmentalism (everything living is interconnected; there is no such thing as a free lunch) as a legitimate way of perceiving the world. Where we once dumped waste anywhere and anytime, where once our factories put tons of pollutants into the air with no concerns, today that is unthinkable. And an entire industry has sprung up to help deal with pollution.

- The rise of the third world as a global influence

- Terrorism as an everyday activity

- Rampant inflation in the U.S.

- Deregulation of
    ...banking
    ...the airlines
    ...telecommunications
    ...trucking

- The loss of the United States' position as the leading edge manufacturer of the world. All of a sudden we find U.S. products not the "premium" products in the world market but third and even fourth behind Japan, Europe, and Korea.

- The new price of energy and new controllers of that price

- The acknowledgment of Japan as a new industrial model

- The growth of participatory management

- The loss of respect for major institutions such as
  ...the Supreme Court
  ...the police
  ...the federal government
  ...the congress

- The loss of union power

- The emergence of information as a key resource

- The loss of a college degree as guarantor of a good job

- Public language on TV and radio incorporating cursing and strong sexual connotation within normal programming

- Cohabitation as an acceptable substitute for marriage

- Growing percentage of Hispanics in the southern U.S.

- The collapse of nuclear power as a viable energy option for the U.S.

- A new appreciation of "small is beautiful" and the rejection of "big is always better." Who would have believed in the '60s that steel minimills would outperform and outcompete the giant mills of U.S. Steel (now USX) and return 20 percent on investment?

And it goes on...

- The common use of satellite communications

- The disappearance of the idea that continuous growth is automatically good

- The vast amount of data exchanged via computers worldwide

- The "uncloseting" of gays and other previously hidden minorities

- The new importance of the role of women in all phases of life including business and politics

- The dominance of energy conservation as a new attitude in the U.S.

- Television as an active screen for games and information rather than just passive entertainment

- The number of people getting regular aerobic exercise every day

- Japan as a producer of the highest quality products

- The number of people eating a healthy diet by choice

- Zero population growth as the norm in the U.S.

- The explosion of personal computers in the home and at the office

- Republicans saying a large federal deficit is okay

There are still many more, but the point is this: we have gone through extraordinary changes in the last twenty years in terms of the alteration of the old rules and regulations of our lives.

Now, let me ask a pragmatic question: What if you had been able to anticipate some of these changes? What if you had known, for sure, about just one of these major changes? What would you have been able to do with that information?

For instance, what if you had anticipated the growth of personal computers? Let's say you did it in 1976 when it was still only a gleam in two college dropouts' eyes. Think of the investment opportunities you could have had.

Or how about the move toward healthy, less fattening foods like yogurt? Who would have guessed it would become so popular?

No matter who you are or what you do, it would have made a big difference. At the very least you would have been subject to less surprise, less "future shock." At the very most, I think it is fair to conclude that you could have made millions of dollars—perhaps even billions of dollars—if you had had that knowledge. The leverage of discovering these kinds of changes is profound, because these kinds of rule changes are **not** predicted by trends. That's why, for many people, even (and, in some case, especially) the experts, they seem "unpredictable."

The fact is that these kinds of changes in the rules create trends or dramatically alter trends already in place. That makes them very special.

Let's get back to the word "anticipate" for a moment. Anticipation is the ability to foresee, to realize beforehand. Peter Drucker, in *Managing in Turbulent Times* (Harper and Row, 1980), makes a very interesting observation. He writes about the skills that a good manager needs and suggests that one of the most important managerial skills during times of high turbulence is **anticipation**.

I strongly support his observation. Take a look at the graph on the following page. What you will find is that almost everyone who is successful in their life's work has strong problem-solving skills, predominantly in the **reactive** mode. That is, when a real problem occurs, we solve it. While we spend most of our time problem solving, we do, once in a while, reach into the other quadrants. But the dominant way we run our lives is in the problem-solving/reaction mode.

What Drucker is suggesting is that we must improve our skills in the opposite quadrant of the grid; that is the area of anticipation/problem avoidance and

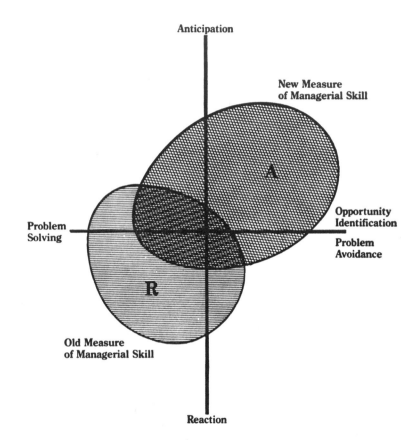

Figure 1. Managerial Skill Domains

opportunity identification. It is in this area that great leverage over the future can be generated – personally, corporately, nationally.

Drucker's point on managing in turbulent times is extremely important. I have a metaphor that illustrates his point in a different way. Think of a river: smooth, crystalline, sandy bottomed, sandy shored, slow, steady flowing. If someone said to you, "Look, I want you to get from this side of the river to the other side of the river," it wouldn't be much of a challenge. All you would need to do is find a boat and a way to power the boat. The point is, to cross a river like that doesn't take much anticipation, because all the information you need is unambiguously in front of you.

Now, let's think about a different river, a highly turbulent one. It is filled with whirlpools and eddies and changes in the current. Because of its turbulence, it has churned up much dirt from the bottom so the water is opaque. It is filled with boulders which can't be seen. The shores on both sides have been eroded by the turbulence and are rocky and irregular. If someone asks you to go from one side of this river to the other, it is fundamentally a different proposition. Here, in fact, **anticipation** will make a big difference in your success. If you can anticipate the rocks below the water, if you can anticipate the whirlpools and the changes in the current, if you can anticipate the take-off from one rocky shore and the landing on the other, you have a much better chance of getting across that river successfully.

10

The times we are living in are much like the turbulent river. And, what I am saying, and what Peter Drucker says, is that, **in times of turbulence, the ability to anticipate enhances, dramatically, your chances of success.**

But, to say that one should anticipate better doesn't explain how to anticipate. You need to understand that:

Good anticipation is the result of good exploration.

If you want to anticipate the future, then you need to be good at **strategic exploration.** With strategic exploration, you can discover the future, and, once you have found out what is possible, you are in position to anticipate it. Exploration leads to discovery, which improves anticipation.

There are five components to strategic exploration:

1. **Influence Understanding**
   The ability to be able to understand what influences our perceptions as we set out on our explorations.

2. **Divergent Thinking**
   The thinking skills necessary for discovering more than one right answer.

3. **Convergent Thinking**
   The thinking skills that allow the focused integration of the data and the prioritizing of choices.

4. Mapping
The capacity to draw pathways from the present to the future.

5. Imaging
The ability to picture in words or drawings what you found in your explorations.

The complete strategic explorer can do all of those things.

This book focuses on the first component, **Influence Understanding.** Because, if you don't understand how your perceptions of the future are influenced, all the other components are useless.

The ability to anticipate comes as a result of good strategic exploration. Some anticipation can be scientific, but the most important aspect of anticipation is artistic. And, just like the artist, practice and persistence will dramatically improve your abilities. Your improved ability will, in turn, increase your leverage to deal with the new worlds coming. As I said several years ago—

"You can and should shape your own future. Because, if you don't, someone else surely will."

That ought to be reason enough to improve your skills.

2

Paradigms

Most of the changes on the list in chapter one were driven by a special phenomenon – a change in **paradigms** (pronounced pair-a-dimes). And, in the jargon of futurists, they would be called "paradigm shifts."

The concept of paradigms and paradigm shifts can help you better understand the nature of these changes. Being able to understand what made them occur will give you a better chance to anticipate them. Remember how much leverage you could have gained had you known about them sooner.

What is a paradigm? If you look up the Greek root, you discover it comes from "paradeigma," which means "model, pattern."

Let me give you some definitions that have appeared in various books since 1962. From:

The Structure of Scientific Revolutions (University of Chicago Press, 1962). Its author, Thomas S. Kuhn, a scientific historian, who revolutionized his field and who brought the concept of the paradigm shift to the scientific world, wrote that scientific paradigms are "...accepted examples of actual scientific practice – examples which include law, theory, application, and instrumentation together – [that] provide models from which spring particular coherent traditions of scientific research." And he adds, "Men whose research is based on shared paradigms are committed to the same rules and standards for scientific practice." (p. 10)

Powers of the Mind (Ballantine Books, 1975) by Adam Smith. Smith is the pen name of a Wall Street economist who wrote *The Money Game, Supermoney*, and *Paper Money*, all best-sellers. He is an excellent researcher and in this book he examines what we have discovered about the mind. His definition is: "A shared set of assumptions. The paradigm is the way we perceive the world; water to the fish. The paradigm explains the world to us and helps us to predict its behavior. When we are in the middle of the paradigm, it is hard to imagine any other paradigm." (p. 19)

In *An Incomplete Guide to the Future* (Norton, 1970), author Willis Harmon, who was was one of the key leaders at the Stanford Research Institute and is now president of the Institute for Noetic Sciences, wrote that a paradigm was: "The basic way of perceiving, thinking, valuing, and doing associated with a particular vision of reality. A dominant paradigm is seldom if ever stated explicitly; it exists as unquestioned, tacit understanding that is transmitted through culture and to succeeding generations through direct experience rather than being taught.... A dominant paradigm encompasses more than an ideology or a world view but less than a total culture." (p. 24)

In *The Aquarian Conspiracy* (Tarcher, 1980), Marilyn Ferguson, who first made her name as editor and publisher of the *Brain/Mind Bulletin*, wrote: "A paradigm is a framework of thought...a scheme for understanding and explaining certain aspects of reality." (p. 26)

Let me offer my definition:

A paradigm is a set of rules and regulations that: 1) defines boundaries; and 2) tells you what to do to be successful within those boundaries. (Success is measured by the problems you solve using these rules and regulations.)

This definition captures the sense of pattern again with the word "boundaries" – these are the edges; these are the borders; this is the pattern. But it also adds the concept of rules and regulations for success. A paradigm, in a sense, tells you **that there is a game, what the game is, and how to play it successfully.** The sense of game is a very appropriate metaphor for paradigms because it reflects the need for borders and directions on how to perform in order to "do it right." A paradigm tells you how to play the game according to the rules. With that definition, you can't help but conclude that there are many paradigms in our everyday life.

A paradigm shift, then, is a change to a new game, a new set of rules.

It is my belief that changes in paradigms are what have been triggering much of society's turbulence for the last twenty years. We had sets of rules we knew well, then someone changed the rules. We understood the old boundaries, then we had to learn new boundaries. And those changes dramatically upset our world.

The best seller of 1982, *Megatrends*, by John Naisbitt, reflects in an indirect way how important paradigm shifts are. Naisbitt suggests that there are ten important new trends that will generate profound changes in our society in the next fifteen to thirty years. I believe that, if you trace back to the beginning of those trends, you will find a paradigm shift. What Naisbitt identifies for us in *Megatrends* is important, because he shows us a pathway of change which we can follow through time to measure how we are getting more of something or less of something; for instance, more decentralization, less centralization in organizational structures in the United States. But, even more important than the pathway is to understand what triggered that change in the first place. What we find is that, at the beginning of the trend, someone created a new set of rules. The decentralization trend is an excellent example of a paradigm shift. The old rules, the old game, was "centralize the organization and make the hierarchy complex." But that game ultimately created big problems. Then somebody discovered that there was a different way to deal with the problems, which was to decentralize the organization; in other words, to change the rules. And the result was a paradigm shift.

As a futurist looking at what kinds of changes are most important to examine, I conclude that:

While trends are important, they are almost always instigated by a paradigm shift. By understanding the way paradigms change, we can better anticipate the future.

3

The Setting
for the Shift

My first exposure to the concept of paradigm shifts came in 1973 when I read Thomas Kuhn's book, *The Structure of Scientific Revolutions*. In it, Kuhn examines how the scientific disciplines shifted their paradigms during the past 400 years. As I read it, I began to understand that his concept was far broader than the scientific context in which it was set. I began to see why so many people in power had been so wrong over the last twenty years and why those same people were unable to identify and understand the major changes that were occurring. If the last twenty years have been marked by anything, they have been marked by the experts repeatedly missing important changes.

So, when we look back to the '60s, we see paradigm shifts: The reason the environmentalists had such a tough time getting their ideas accepted was because they were offering a paradigm shift; parents responded so violently to drugs and long hair on their children because it was a paradigm shift; we missed the OPEC revolution because of a paradigm shift. Our country's inability to understand the Iranian revolution had to do with paradigms. And I believe much of the confusion we have about the future is because of changes in paradigms.

These paradigm changes are expecially important for all of us because, whether it is in business or education or politics or personal life, a paradigm change, by definition, alters the basic rules of the game.

And, when the rules change, the whole world can change.

The points that Kuhn makes about scientific paradigm shifts I claim are true for any situation where strongly held rules and regulations exist.

Obviously Kuhn says much more about scientific paradigms and with wonderful depth. I should also add one more thing which is a clear disclaimer: I doubt very much if Kuhn appreciates the extent to which I, and others, have generalized his concepts. In his book he states that only in science, where the rules and examples and measures are precise, can paradigms exist. And only with that subtlety and accuracy that science has can changes in paradigms be measured so as to trigger the search for a new paradigm. So I accept the obligation imposed by Kuhn's own careful qualification. In spite of Kuhn's argument to the contrary I still believe that his observations can be applied in a broader sense with great utility. I hope you will find this true as well.

To direct our discussion, we will focus on four questions. Each question deals with a specific aspect of paradigm shifts that will allow us to better anticipate their change. The remainder of this chapter focuses on the first question.

Question 1: What triggers the creation of a new paradigm?

Question 2: What kind of person is a paradigm shifter?

Question 3: Who are the early followers of the paradigm shifter (I call them paradigm pioneers), and why?

Question 4: How does a paradigm shift affect those who go through it?

To begin, then: what are the conditions that trigger a paradigm shift?

I think it is best to think of the development of a paradigm on the lines of an S-shaped curve, with the X axis Time, and the Y axis Problems Solved (figure 2). This line has two inflections. The turning up of the line indicates that the paradigm is now understood well enough to become an efficient and effective problem-solving system. The second change in the line slope indicates the maturation of the paradigm, when it is running out of problems and/or it is left with extremely difficult and sophisticated problems so that the time-per-problem-solved becomes increasingly longer.

When is the logical time to seek a new paradigm?

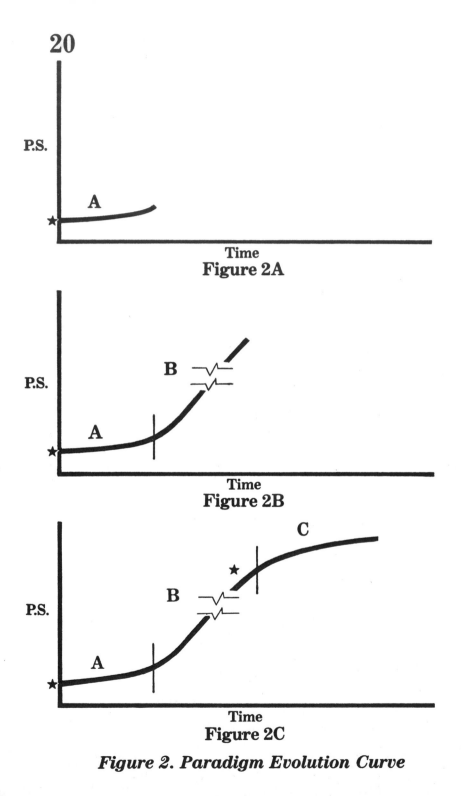

Figure 2A

Figure 2B

Figure 2C

Figure 2. Paradigm Evolution Curve

The logical answer is in segment C. The need is clear; the cost is clear. The fear of running out of problems to solve would be a rational driving force.

But the correct answer to the question is during the latter part of segment B. Why? In his book, Kuhn explains it this way: as scientists apply their paradigm to new problems they solve many of them. But even though they are very successful and solve many problems, they do not solve all the problems they attempt. While they would like to solve all the problems, a few unsolved ones do not bother them too much, at least not at first. Usually they have explanations for why they cannot solve them. For instance, one explanation goes like this:

"I haven't practiced the paradigm long enough to know exactly how to solve this problem; therefore, I will put it on a shelf. Five years from now, I will come back when I am wiser, when I am more sophisticated at using these rules, and then I will solve the problem."

And the problem is put on a shelf to wait for a more sophisticated problem solver.

There is another explanation which has to do with technology:

"I can't solve this problem because I can't see far enough or weigh finely enough or measure as precisely as I need—my supporting technology is inadequate."

The inability to solve these special problems becomes a question not of the practitioner's skills but the power of the equipment. And so, again, they put these problems on a shelf to wait for the technology to be developed.

Please note that both explanations are legitimate. For instance, until we had Boeing 707s and atomic clocks, we could not perform certain tests on Einstein's theory of relativity measuring how time was affected by speed. Once we had those two pieces of technology, we could and did. (The results indicated Einstein was right.)

So practitioners of scientific paradigms have two legitimate excuses for unsolved problems, "We're not clever enough yet," and "We don't have the right support equipment yet." The result: problems go up on a shelf and wait to be solved.

It turns out that these excuses are good for, not just scientists, but all paradigm practioners. Think of the kinds of problems business people were able to solve when they could use the new computerized spread sheets. Without those new software tools, whole categories of problems remained unapproachable, even though the business paradigm theoretically could deal with those problems.

Over time, many of these problems do get solved; a wiser person, a better piece of equipment makes the difference. But, other problems come down from the shelf to be solved only to be put back up. They begin to earn a special reputation for impossibility. Neither wisdom nor technology allows their solution, and these kinds of problems, accumulating slowly but steadily, are frustrating puzzles for the prevailing paradigm community. The paradigm somehow does not seem to give them the power to solve these problems.

Let me give you a nonscientific example of how a set of these problems plague a paradigm. The legal field has a shelf full of seemingly insoluble problems that has grown to impressive size over the past few years. Here are just three of problems from that shelf that look like they have no solutions within the prevailing paradigm:

• A turtle-slow movement of cases through the court systems coupled to endless rounds of appeals. Justice delayed by endless routines.

• The cost of defense. Only the well-off can afford to defend themselves adequately. How can that be justice?

• An ongoing pattern of no negotiations except in the courts with all-or-nothing strategies and gigantic settlement requests.

Yet most lawyers would have perfectly valid explanations for these problems. They would suggest that while these problems are troublesome they will not destroy the system.

Still, while the impossible problems accumulate on the shelf, the practitioners of the established paradigm continue to solve many other problems. So the special problems are not perceived as a measure of failure, only incompleteness. Yet, quietly, relentlessly, their presence pushes toward a critical mass that will ultimately trigger change.

Please note: the prevailing paradigm is still successful. What Kuhn points out for the scientific community is that the critical mass of unsolved problems creates a quiet uncertainty within the community. And that uncertainty increases the likelihood that certain kinds of people might begin to look for a paradigm to replace the old. So, we are now at a point where the triggering mechanism is in place for the search for the new paradigm. If we want to locate that place on our curve it is probably somewhere within the latter part of segment B. The seeds of succession begin to germinate while the old paradigm is still vigorous. The trigger is the critical mass of special problems waiting to stimulate the mind of the "paradigm shifter." And this critical mass is usually created while the paradigm is still doing well.

The generalization from this first observation is very important for established paradigm communities. To keep track of the important unsolved problems is a way of monitoring the critical mass. When the community starts talking in frustrated ways about those problems, it is an indication of willingness to search for other alternatives. And, if you feel your paradigm has moved into the C segment of its development, you should look around to see if its replacement has not already been discovered!

Now the question is—Who is it that discovers new paradigms?

4 *Enter the "Shifter"*

It is at this point, as the shelf is beginning to fill up with these special problems, that the **paradigm shifter** enters the picture. So let us now answer the second question:

What kind of person is a paradigm shifter?

The short answer is simple: **an outsider.** Kuhn writes that in science the person who is most likely to begin to create new rules rather than just apply the old rules is from one of two backgrounds and my own work over the past decade in other fields confirms his and adds a third:

1) A young graduate, newly out of school, who has been trained in the field but has not practiced in it. (And we all know the difference between training and practice.) Young Albert Einstein illustrates this perfectly in physics.

2) An older scientist who is shifting fields: i.e., he or she was in chemistry and got tired of chemistry and decided to go into biology; was in biology and got tired of that and decided to go into physics, etc. The point is this: the scientist is moving from a field he or she knows well into a new field. A perfect example is Dr. Alex Mueller, Nobel Prize co-winner in 1987 for his discovery of superconducting ceramics. He was a physicist but didn't practice in the field of superconducting. Let me quote from the *Wall Street Journal* article of August 19, 1987: Said Dr. Mueller, " 'I was a greenhorn and an outsider' in the specialized field of superconducting."

My own work looking at fields other than science continues to reaffirm Kuhn's description – young, unpracticed; older, shifting fields.

Fred Smith, the founder of Federal Express, illustrates this phenomenon in business. He was "out of line" at his young age to start such a revolutionary package-carrier-and-delivery system. He had written a paper on his idea in college and was told by his wizened professors that it was an unworkable and unnecessary idea.

The quality that both of these two types share is **operational naiveté** about the field. They don't understand many of the subtle aspects of the paradigm community they want to join.

There is another characteristic that these two share which makes them different from practitioners of the prevailing paradigm: **they lack investment in the**

old paradigm. They have garnered neither status nor monetary remuneration for practicing the established paradigm. And, since they are not invested in the old rules, they have little to lose by creating a new set of rules.

There is also a third kind of paradigm shifter that I have identified who is not mentioned by Kuhn, mainly because this person is outside Kuhn's realm. This person can best be described as a **tinkerer**.

The key characteristic of tinkerers is that they fix problems that have become important to them. Often they don't care about paradigms or communities. They have simply run into a problem (which happens to be one of those special problems on the shelf) that they need to solve. It is irrelevant to them that the problem may be one of a set of important unsolved problems of some paradigm. They just work on their problem until they solve it. And, in the process, they accidently create a new paradigm, which will solve not only their specific problem but a class of problems. But, for the tinkerer, their job is done when they have solved the single problem that was bothering them. It has been noted that scientists sometimes are stimulated to discover a new paradigm trying to explain the results of tinkerers. When they look at the solution the tinkerer has to offer, their initial reaction is "Well, that's impossible." But, upon further examination, they discover that the tinkerer has, indeed, found a new way to solve problems.

Look who revolutionized accounting by developing an electronic spread sheet? Some whiz kid from Arthur

Andersen? A veteran from Ernst & Whinney? Or some famous Ph.D. at the Michigan State business school? Nope. It was a young computer programmer who knew precious little about accounting. But he did have this great idea he called Visicalc and as he created it, he kept an accounting textbook beside him to make sure he was doing it right. A clear case of tinkering.

The Bell System was revolutionized in the late 1800s by a tinker. His name was Almond B. Strowger. He invented and patented the rotary dialing system. His profession: undertaker.

That sounds like an outsider, for starters, doesn't it? Why would an undertaker invent a telephone switch? Because he had a problem. When telephones came to Kansas City where he lived, his business dropped from 50 percent to almost 0. Of course, he immediately began to investigate the cause of his problem and found that the operator of the system happened to be the wife of the other undertaker. And, when someone called for the undertaker, she always connected the party to her husband.

Mr. Strowger tried to convince her to be more fair-minded but she would have none of it. So, in desperation, he began to think of ways his potential customers could reach him without having to connect first through her.

His solution was the rotary-dialing concept and the switching mechanism that would make it all work. His solution to his problem was a solution to an enormous number of problems and even today in many parts of the world the results of his tinkering are still in use.

All three types of paradigm shifters have zero credibility with the prevailing paradigm community. That's why it's so easy to ignore them. That's why they surprise us so often.

Let us return to Kuhn's two types of shifters. These scientists want to join the paradigm community. One of the ways to demonstrate one's worthiness is to solve some problems, so they look around for some interesting problems to work on. By definition, the most interesting problems are the unsolved ones sitting on the shelf. And, if a newcomer solves one of those problems, he or she will have immediate entry into the paradigm community. There is no quicker way to gain prestige and power than to solve one of those unsolved problems…**if you use the prevailing paradigm to do it!**

The uninvested scientists always try applying the old rules to the problems first. But soon they discover what everyone else already knows. These are tough problems. They are not able to solve these problems with those rules. Now, at this point, most of them turn away from the problems on the shelf and go looking for some problems the prevailing paradigm will solve.

But a few stubborn, creative ones respond to their lack of success in a fundamentally different way. They dare to speculate, "These aren't the right rules for solving these problems!" And, with that barrier broken, they boldly search for a different set of rules, a new paradigm, that will allow them to solve the problems.

Obviously, almost all of this group fails, too. It is an act of great creativity to fabricate a successful new paradigm. But, every once in a while, an individual does come up with a new set of rules that looks promising. To test it, the creator applies it to one of the problems sitting on the shelf...and solves it! He or she applies it to another problem and solves that one, too! Then another, and another! It looks like a breakthrough!

After a little more testing of the new approach, the paradigm shifter turns to the prevailing paradigm community and says with great sincerity and enthusiasm, "Hey! Look at this! If you would just use these rules I've created instead of yours, you could solve these unsolvable problems!"

What a wonderful offer! What a great gesture! However...

I am sure you can guess the reception they receive. It is almost always the same. And the responses they hear are universal:

"Why that's impossible!"

"We don't do things that way!"

"It's too radical a change."

"We tried something like that before, and it didn't work."

"We would be the laughing stock!"

"I wish it were that easy."

"It's against accepted policy."

"I always thought you were a little weird."

"Who told you you could change the rules?"

"Let's get back to reality."

"How dare you suggest that what we're doing is wrong."

and the archetypical response:

"If you had been in this field as long as I have, you would know that what you are suggesting is absolutely absurd!"

Even though these responses seem grossly unfair, they turn out to be, upon examination, legitimate and logical. For instance, if you were to measure quantitatively who has solved the larger number of problems, the scale will **always** tip in favor of the old paradigm. People have been using the old paradigm because, with it, they could solve problems; therefore, they have hundreds, even thousands, of problems solved using their rules. The person suggesting the new rules has three? four? eight solutions? Certainly not many. Who has the better quantitative measure? **Always the old.**

There's a second reason for that rejection, though this has more to do with emotional commitment than it has to do with logic. If you had been developing and applying a paradigm for thirty years and had gained your status and your security because of your ability to solve problems with the old rules, how would you feel if somebody came along who didn't even have experience in the field and said, "By the way, your entire approach is wrong!"? It is unlikely that you would respond, "Oh, thank you very much, I didn't realize that. Quick, let me change." The more honest response is, "Who the hell do you think you are?"

New paradigms put everyone practicing the old paradigm at great risk. And, the higher one's position, the greater the risk. The better you are at your paradigm, the more you have invested in it. To change your paradigm is to lose that investment.

The implications of the nature of paradigm shifters can be applied broadly. How often has an important innovation in technology, or business, or education, or any field where there are rules and regulations, come from the established practitioners? Rarely. If you are doing well using the old paradigm, it makes no sense whatsoever to turn around and put yourself out of business by creating a new set of rules. No! It makes much more sense for you to continue to practice the old paradigm.

So, where is the logical place for innovation to come from? The edges, the fringes, where there are outsiders who do not know that "it can't be done."

Remember outsiders have no investment in the old paradigm, so they have nothing to lose by changing it.

When I was in Toronto in 1982, James Watson, co-discoverer with Francis Crick of the DNA biological paradigm, was being interviewed on TV. The interviewer asked how it came to be that he, Watson, instead of somebody else, made this great discovery. Watson's statement rings true in terms of what I have just stated. He answered,

> **"Well, you see, I was doing something my peers thought unwise; if they had thought it wise, they would have done it."**

A perfect articulation of a paradigm shifter.

5 The Paradigm Pioneers

What's the difference between a pioneer and a settler? It is the settler who is always calling out over the horizon, "Is it safe out there now?" The voice they hear coming back is the pioneer's, "Of course, it's safe out here." That's because the pioneers took the risk, went out early, and made it safe.

Paradigm shifters need paradigm pioneers to help them bring about the change. It is time to answer question 3: **Who are the early followers of the paradigm shifters?**

To answer this question, we need to ask another, first: what is the attitude of the prevailing paradigm community following the initial rejection of the new paradigm?

The attitude in the paradigm community is continued disbelief of the new paradigm by many but growing frustration and quiet questioning by some. The paradigm shifter is a catalyst, a change agent, and part of the role of a catalyst is to stir things up. What the paradigm shifter has offered is an alternative way of thinking about the anomalous problems. While that is initially very uncomfortable for the paradigm community because it messes up its pleasant environment, it ultimately leads to constructive, but quiet, criticism. The prevailing paradigm practitioners really do want to solve those unsolvable problems, and a few are now challenged to think about a new and different set of rules. If the paradigm is a good one, sooner or later some will say to themselves:

"You know, the more I think about these rules, the more interesting they are."

"There's something clever about the way these rules approach those problems."

"There's a kind of elegance to this approach."

"I don't know what it is, but there's something going on here."

These quiet musings articulate a special kind of judgment about the new paradigm. This evaluation is **not** a quantitative evaluation; there aren't enough data to be measured meaningfully. Instead, the judgment on the correctness of the new paradigm is based on intuition, gut-level reaction, a gestalt of the situation to judge the new paradigm. Based on a **feeling** about the rightness of the paradigm, some choose to switch over.

And it is these people who are the pioneers of the new paradigm.

Let me quote from Kuhn because he says it so well.

The man who embraces a new paradigm at an early stage must often do so in defiance of the evidence provided by the problem solving. He must, that is, have faith that the new paradigm will succeed with the many large problems that confront it knowing only that the older paradigm has failed with a few. A decision of that kind can only be made on faith (pp. 157–58).

The essence of this is:

Those who choose to change their paradigms early do it not as an act of the head but as an act of the heart.

Titillated by a set of rules that suggests they may be able to succeed where before they failed, these pioneers risk their reputations, their positions, even their economic situations on a **non-rational** decision. It is the aesthetic appeal of the new paradigm, the beauty with which it appears to solve problems, rather than quantitative proof of problem-solving that precipitates the decision to change. Driven by the frustration of the old and the appeal of the new, they cross the brink: they leap across a professional chasm that separates the old paradigm, where the territory is well illuminated and where their reputations and positions are clearly defined, into a new territory, illuminated by the new paradigm in such a limited way that it is impossible to have any idea whether or not they are standing on the edge of an unexplored continent or merely a tiny island.

This choice to change from the old paradigm to the new paradigm early in its development is extremely risky and takes great courage. These pioneers know that if this new paradigm dead-ends or turns out to have a limited area of discovery available, they will have a very difficult time going back to the old community. The returning pioneer, if not an outcast, will have significantly lower status – "Oh, it's you. Weren't you the one who told us you were going to join the new group and revolutionize the field?"

Non-rational decision-making and courage: those are the two hallmarks of a leader. And can you think of anyplace where leadership is required more than the changing of paradigms? Leaders are willing to take a risk.

This great risk, however, is balanced with tremendous opportunity: if it turns out that the new paradigm is one with depth and breadth, those who change early have the first crack at all the territory. And if they have enough talent, they are bound to solve significant problems.

Look at the risk the United States took when it committed to spending hundreds of billions of dollars on reducing pollution before all the facts were in. Had it turned out that the environmentalists were wrong, all that expense would have had, not only no value, but devastating negative impacts on the nation's capital needs.

Europe, on the other hand, decided to wait for the facts, chose to be a settler. The facts came in the mid-'80s by way of 30 percent of the trees in the Black Forest dead or dying from pollution. That made them take action. Now they will have to spend the money for pollution equipment and pay to correct the environmental damage that would have been minimized had they joined with the United States as pioneers.

IBM, believe it or not, took a pioneering position to bring out their personal computer. Remember that the decision to enter the market was made before there was a significant base of data to prove the correctness of the decision. So IBM pioneered the PC revolution. Had it not worked out, they would have lost credibility. Instead their entry proved to the rest of the industry that there really was a new, yet-to-be-unexplored territory in the computer world.

So there is an important trade-off that goes with being a paradigm pioneer. While there is great risk, there is a tremendous potential for professional reward. This trade-off is especially important for new ventures in business. Being early into a new field offers an economic benefit: the cost of exploration is often much cheaper earlier than it will be later on. As the paradigm gains in sophistication, it requires more technology, more laboratories, more time and personnel, to discover and solve the more sophisticated problems.

So, first in – big risk; first in – big potential leverage. That is the trade-off for the paradigm pioneer.

For me, this aspect of the paradigm change is especially interesting because of what it says about the objectivity of science. The most important time for the scientific community, when the pioneers choose its new rules and commit to them, is a **non-rational** time. It has to be. So even science, which strives for rationality and objectivity, has its non-rational, subjective time, and that time is one of the most important times of scientific activity.

In this discussion is a special message for all pioneers. If you want to be one of the first into the new territory, you cannot wait for large amounts of evidence. In fact, you have to do exactly the opposite. If you are to be early, you must trust your intuition, you must trust your non-rational judgment and take the plunge; make the leap of faith to the new paradigm. If you wait until the facts are irrefutable, you will be merely a settler and it will be too late to gain any special advantage.

6

The Paradigm Effect

So far, we understand that:

1) the prevailing paradigm triggers the search for a new paradigm while it is still successful by identifying enough anomalies, "unsolvable" problems, to create a critical mass;

2) paradigm shifters are usually outsiders who come from the fringes, not the center of the prevailing paradigm community; and

3) pioneers, who accept the new paradigm early, will never have enough proof to make that acceptance a rational judgment. They will choose to follow because of their trust in their intuition.

Now, for the fourth question which focuses on the results of experiencing a paradigm shift. It is, for me, the **most important question** about paradigms. It illuminates the single most important aspect of paradigms and their influence on our ability to explore the future.

How do paradigm shifts affect those who go through them?

Kuhn noticed an unusual kind of statement that occurred in the writings of those who changed their paradigms. Frequently he came across phrases that had a nonscientific flavor to them, a kind of exaggerated description; phrases like, "The scales have fallen from my eyes." Such phrases indicated that the scientists seemed to be seeing things that they had not seen before.

Why would thoughtful and conscientious scientists use such language? It was not the language of precision or objectivity. A logical explanation would be simply that the new paradigm forced them to look in a different direction. And, since they were looking in a different direction, they had no choice but to see things they never saw before.

But that is not what Kuhn concluded because he came across situations where the scientists were reproducing, as exactly as possible, old experiments – same subject, same controls, same method of observation, and were still writing about seeing something totally new. The only change in the experiment was their paradigm.

Let me quote Kuhn:

In a sense that I am unable to explicate further, the

proponents of competing paradigms practiced their trades in different worlds...**Practicing in different worlds, the two groups of scientists see different things when they look from the same point in the same direction** [my emphasis]. Again, that is not to say they can see anything they please. Both are looking at the world, and what they look at has not changed. But, in some areas, they see different things, and they see them in different relations one to the other. That is why a law that cannot even be demonstrated to one group of scientists may seem intuitively obvious to another. (p. 150)

What Kuhn suggests here, and I would carry even further, is that when a scientist changes his paradigm, he is empowered by the new rules to be able to perceive things in the world that he was unable to perceive before.

Let me put that even more strongly. I think what Kuhn is saying is that paradigms act as **physiological filters**–that we see the world quite literally through our paradigms.

Let me reiterate this. A paradigm acts as an information filter, and what we actually perceive is determined by our paradigms. What may be perfectly visible, perfectly obvious, to persons with one paradigm may be **quite literally invisible** to persons with a different paradigm.

And this is the **paradigm effect**.

In 1973, when I came to this point in Kuhn's book, I remember sitting back and understanding a decade of wrong decisions. I had watched people I thought were intelligent make decisions which turned out to be terrible. I couldn't figure out how they had missed them all.

For instance, the tremendous resistance by big business to the environmentalists. I had thought the business leaders were just stupid, or arrogant, or too consumed with making money. And I am sure that was part of the resistance. But more of the resistance, I am now convinced, was simply a true inability to see what the environmentalists were pointing out. Their old paradigms blocked their ability to perceive and understand what was really happening out there in the world.

Today, the vast majority of business people, even those who were part of the initial resistance, would agree uncategorically that the environment must be protected.

General Motors had the same kind of problem with Ralph Nader. They didn't get it. And "not getting it" meant that Nader's consumer-rights position couldn't get through their filters so they were unable to understand.

Remember the father-son battles over length of hair in the '60s? We laugh at it today, but it was serious business in those days. It was a redefinition of "maleness" and the dads with old rules couldn't handle it.

The same was true of the demographers' response to Paul Ehrlich's plea for Zero Population Growth–ZPG. A top demographer, Ben Wattenberg, would appear on *Meet the Press* and say things like, "The U.S. will never reduce its birth rate." Because that was just the way things were – based on his paradigm. Today we are practicing ZPG.

The list goes on and on, and it indicates two things: how powerfully paradigms can trap us into seeing the world in only one way; and how wrong experts can be because of that entrapment.

I realized that the leaders who were making those bad decisions were not making them because they were stupid or uneducated or malicious. They were making them because they were trying to apply old paradigms to situations where a new paradigm was emerging. And, since 1973, the list demonstrating this dilemma has grown much longer. I now understand that if one is to be able to explore the future well, the most important thing to know is how much influence our paradigms exert on our perception of the world around us.

Understanding the paradigm effect is the key step in becoming a successful strategic explorer.

Since then, I have also had the opportunity to talk to people who saw parallels to this phenomenon in linguistics, anthropology, cognitive psychology, and many other fields. Kuhn's observation in science brought a sweeping understanding of the magnitude of this phenomenon.

The importance of Kuhn's book is that he brings a pivotal group into the discussion. Sociologists describe the effect in fanatics, anthropologists describe the effect in cultures; Kuhn showed that **even scientists** could be dramatically influenced by their paradigms, They have no special immunity from this kind of influence on their perception!

A paradigm, then, is like a two-edged sword. When swung the "right" way, it cuts the world into discrete bits of refined information which gives the paradigm practitioner very subtle vision. That's the good side of the paradigm.

But when the sword is swung the "wrong" way, it cuts the user **away** from information that runs counter to the paradigm. At best the user will write off the information as "impossible" or "inaccurate," and, at worst, will be incapable of perceiving the information at all!

To put this paradigm effect into a positive light let me suggest that we can dramatically improve our exploratory skills by knowing consciously how our present paradigms interfere with our perceptions of the future.

What is defined as "impossible" today is impossible only in the context of present paradigms.

To see the future more clearly, we must put aside our certainties in our present rules and regulations and begin to examine the fringes for the people who are changing the paradigms.

By understanding the paradigm effect, we can lift ourselves above its power to blind and begin to search for the new rules.

7

Nine Examples

Up to this point, I have been talking about an abstraction. If this book is to have any value, it must be illustrated with concrete examples. That is what this chapter is about. I'm going to offer you nine examples of the power and influence of paradigms. I have more than 200 of these examples in my files, but, if these don't convince you, none of the others will either.

Each of these examples illustrates some of the key aspects to paradigm shifts: 1) the birth of the new paradigm during the success of the old; 2) the paradigm shifter as outsider; and 3) the blinding effects of paradigms on their users. I do not take the time to track the history of all the paradigm pioneers, but it could easily be done in those examples where it is appropriate.

I have selected nine examples to demonstrate how widely this idea of paradigm shift and paradigm influence is. It is my experience that once you begin to see how applicable the concept is, you will begin to find examples from your own experience which will also illustrate what I have been describing.

Vision Askew

At the Hanover Institute in Germany in the late 1800s, the following experiment was done. Subjects were asked to put on goggles that had inverting lenses in them. That is, when the subjects looked through the lenses, the world appeared upside down. The purpose of the research was to see how subjects responded to this unusual situation.

Now, if you or I were asked to speculate on the ways the subjects might respond to this predicament we would probably guess that they would learn to adjust to "upsidedownness." (However, we would also worry about these goggled people trying to walk down steps or negotiate street crossings.)

How did the subjects deal with the upside down vision problem? While some took a short time and others took many hours, all who wore the goggles ultimately reported to the experimenters that "the world was back to normal."

Their solution was simple: turn the information rightside up! Somehow they were able to unconsciously search out the vision-control mechanism inside their brains and "click the switch" that turned the information 180 degrees around! That is an amazing solution to the problem.

To put it into paradigm language, when confronted with the choice of creating new rules to deal with the upside-down information or keeping the old rules and altering the information, the subjects of this experiment did the most efficient thing: they kept their rules and changed the data. And that change allowed them to deal with the world efficiently and effectively at minimum disruption to their way of seeing the world.

This simple experiment is a very powerful demonstration of our ability to **manipulate the physiological information coming into our minds.** Who would have guessed that, by choice, we could so dramatically alter our sensory information? We have far more control over what we perceive and how we perceive than we realize.

The Chess Masters

In 1973, Herbert Simon, Nobel Prize winner in economics at Carnegie Mellon University, was studying perception in chess players with William C. Chase. Their study was reported in *Cognitive Psychology*, Vol. IV, pp. 55–81, and it demonstrates the influence of paradigms. The essence of the research was as follows.

Chase and Simon enlisted three chess players with international rankings, three intermediate chess players, and three who were novice players to be their subjects.

Behind a movable partition the experimenters set up a partially played chess game. Then, for each subject, the partition was removed and the subject was given five seconds to look at the board. After five seconds, the partition was replaced and the subject was asked to recreate on a blank chess board as accurately as possible what he had seen during the five seconds.

The contrasting success between the master chess players and novices was the most dramatic. As you might guess the masters did very well, indeed. In fact, the average accuracy, with twenty chess pieces on the board, was 81 percent! That is very impressive recall with just five seconds of observation.

In the same situation, the novice chess players' performances were poor—about 33 percent of the pieces were correctly recalled.

Clearly the difference between the two groups was significant.

Now, if you were to stop the experiment at this point and speculate on the difference, you might come up with several theories:

a. The master players have amazing memories

b. Playing the game well makes you better at remembering

c. The masters have special tricks for recalling the pieces

Chase and Simon then proceeded with the second

part of the experiment. This time, they altered one factor: the chess pieces were arranged **randomly** by computer with no attention paid to the rules of the game. Again, the three different groups of players were given the same amount of time to look at the new set-up. And, again, they were asked to recreate what they saw on empty chess boards.

What happened this time? Surprisingly, the championship chess players' performances collapsed. Their placement accuracy plummeted. To be exact, their placement was reduced to worse than the beginners!

What happened? It has to do with paradigms. The chess paradigm was removed, and, as a result, the subtle and accurate perception of the master chess players, created by long hours of practice and play, was rendered useless. With the rules, they could draw inferences of location and relationship that gave them incredible accuracy. But, once those rules were gone, their subtle vision was eliminated. Their paradigm gave them wonderful vision within the boundaries of the game! When the paradigm was removed, the masters were masters no longer.

How many experts in the last twenty years have been treated just as rudely?

Budweiser Beer Can'ts

The first two examples are useful because they were carefully controlled experiments. But that also is their weakness. We need to examine the paradigm effect in the real world.

In 1977, in Boca Raton, Florida, I was giving the paradigm lecture to a group of IBM managers. Shortly after I finished, a young man from the audience came up and said, "I now understand something I could never explain before." (Words like that are music to my ears!) This was his story:

At that time he was an avid scuba diver. Quite often he dove to the depths of 100–150 feet to check out traps he had outside Miami Beach. Because that area is well-trafficked by expensive yachts, lots of garbage is strewn along the ocean floor, especially beer cans. His problem had been caused by the fact that when he saw Budweiser beer cans down at the 150 foot level, he clearly saw their **red** labels.

Why did that bother him? If you have studied the physics of light, you know that the color red **cannot** penetrate through 150 feet of water. All that you have left at that depth is green and the few other colors far toward the ultraviolet end of the spectrum. There is no color red at that depth! And that is what bothered him. He knew he shouldn't be seeing red.

So, how was he able to see the color that could not be there? He saw the red label because he knew the "paradigm" of the Budweiser beer can. That is, he knew the color it was **supposed to be,** and, in order to make it fit the rules, he literally colored the can in his mind. In reality, that label could not show up as red. But, as far as his perception was concerned, it was Budweiser red.

Since that time, when I've shared his story with some of my audiences, other scuba divers come up afterwards to tell me that they see the coloring of fish at depths where their colors shouldn't register. But, because they know the correct coloring of the fish, they **see** it. One diver said, "When I first see them, usually they don't have much color at all. But, within five to ten seconds, they are as brilliant as I know them to be." Interesting language, "know them to be."

With this example, we see the physiological power of the rules to quite literally add information to reality to make it **right.**

The River Boat Pilot

Paradigm examples appear in surprising places as the beer-can story proves. Three years ago, I was watching a dramatization of *Life on the Mississippi* by Samuel Clemens (Mark Twain) on the Public Broadcasting System. One scene made me sit up and watch intently because the discussion was a beautiful articulation of the influence of paradigms.

The novice river pilot and his friend were watching the sunset, and the friend was waxing poetic about the beauty of the river. But, where the friend saw loveliness, the pilot-in-training saw something very different. After the segment concluded, I went immediately to my library and found the book. It took me fifteen minutes of searching to find the passage from which the scene was created. Let me share it with you as Twain wrote it:

First, the loveliness:

A broad expanse of the river was turning to blood; in the middle distance the red hue brightened into gold, through which a solitary log came floating, black and conspicuous; in one place a long, slanting mark lay sparkling upon the water; in another the surface was broken by boiling, tumbling rings, that were as many-tinted as an opal; where the ruddy flush was faintest, was a smooth spot that was covered with graceful circles and radiating lines, ever so delicately traced....

He concludes:

I stood like one bewitched. I drank it in, in a speechless rapture. The world was new to me, and I had never seen anything like this at home.

But, as he travelled the river learning to pilot, his perception was changed by his education and he reflected on how he would view the same scene from his pilot's point of view:

If that sunset scene had been repeated, I should have looked upon it without rapture, and should have commented upon it, inwardly after this fashion: This sun means that we are going to have wind tomorrow; that floating log means that the river is rising, small thanks to it; that slanting mark on the water refers to a bluff reef which is going to kill somebody's steamboat one of these nights, if it keeps on stretching out like that; those tumbling 'boils' show a dissolving bar and a changing channel there; the lines and circles in the slick water over yonder are a warning that that troublesome place is shoaling up dangerously...

His conclusion to this change of vision reflects the dilemma of any expert: "All the value of any feature of it [the river] had for me now was the amount of usefulness it could furnish toward compassing the safe piloting of a steamboat."

As Kuhn noted, and I am trying to reinforce, when you change your paradigm, or, in the case of Sam Clemens, when you learn a paradigm, the world becomes a different place.

New Photography

The first four examples represent examples that are strongly personal. The next three focus on technology. It is in this area that I have the largest number of examples of the paradigm effect.

This story is something of a myth in corporate circles because so many companies missed a major opportunity.

In the late 1940s, a man walked into one of the laboratories of a major photography company to demonstrate his concept of a new kind of photography. He brought along a bright red box which had inside it a shiny steel plate, a secret charging device, and a lightbulb. He also brought, in a separate container, fine black powder.

In front of a company researcher he carefully went through his process, step by step, explaining what he had done. By the end of his demonstration, he had created, using only his unusual equipment, a faint but perceptible photograph.

Now, the inventor never recorded what was said to him as he finished. But the comments probably focused on lack of film, no developer, no fix, no darkroom! And probably a concluding comment such as, "Why would we possibly be interested in such an invention. It is not really even photography!"

Whatever was said, the company's action was clear: he was treated the way most paradigm shifters are; he was shown to the door. Thanks, but no thanks. Not only did that company reject his idea but so did forty-two others.

Ultimately, the inventor, Chester Carlson, had the last laugh. With the help of the Battelle Corporation, he improved his invention and found a company that was willing to develop his photographic process. It became what we now call Xerography. What Chester Carlson invented was a set of rules and regulations for electrostatic photography. Only the Halloid Corporation, which ultimately changed its name to Xerox Corporation, had the foresight to see that this new paradigm was worthy of commercial development. I am sure IBM and Kodak and all the other companies that turned down Chester Carlson would love to have a second chance.

The Human-Powered Airplane

The name, Dr. Paul D. MacCready, will go down in the history books of aviation for an unusual but wonderful reason. He was the inventor of the first successful human-powered plane. And the paradigm effect was key to his success and others' failures.

It all started with the creation of the Kremer Prize. This prize, originated in England in 1969 and worth 50,000 pounds sterling, was offered to the developers of the first human-powered airplane able to fly a prescribed figure eight course with two turning points not less than one-half mile apart while negotiating a ten-foot-high marker at the starting line and the finish line of the course.

Colleges and universities around the world competed for this prize. Many engineers considered the task impossible. But MacCready put an end to that opinion on August 23, 1977, when his plane, the Gossamer Condor, pedal-powered and piloted by Bryan Allen, flew the course according to the rules.

Kremer immediately created a second competition, this time to fly across the English Channel with human power. Within two years, in response to the prize of 100,000 pounds sterling, MacCready's team did it again, with the Gossamer Albatross.

So, what has this to do with paradigms? In a short article written for *Science Digest*, March, 1983, Mac-Cready explained why it was he and not the specialists in aeronautical engineering who won the prize:

My secret weapon was a complete lack of experience in aircraft-wing structural design while, at the same time, having a familiarity with hang gliders and fragile model airplanes...Our competitors also knew about hang gliders, but they were thwarted by knowing so much about standard techniques.

MacCready suggests that his human-powered plane experience made him begin noticing how often people were stopped from doing things by "barriers that really didn't exist." He writes,

I soon found that a dominant factor in the way our minds work is the buildup of patterns that enable us to simplify the assimilation of complex inputs. But this same patterning can be a weakness as well as a strength. The patterning makes it hard for a new idea to get fair treatment.

Because Paul MacCready had a different set of rules from his competitors who were rigorously trained in the field, he was able to solve the problem with his alternative paradigm.

Again and again, we see this in technological settings.

Watching Out for Change

Sometimes technological paradigms and management paradigms intermingle. The story of the development of the quartz watch is a perfect example.

I wear a quartz timepiece. Often I hold up my left arm and ask my audiences, "Who invented the quartz watch?"

The standard answers are:

- the Japanese
- Texas Instruments
- chip makers

And, then, one other answer is almost always given by someone, "For sure, **not** the Swiss!"

The audience chuckles at the last comment, because we all know how badly the Swiss have been hurt by the advent of the quartz watch. They are only now making a substantial push back into the watch marketplace that they once dominated.

The quartz-watch revolution – read paradigm shift – destroyed the Swiss hold on the market, which was as high as 90 percent before World War II and still 60 percent in the '70s. By the early 1980s their market share was below 10 percent.

The employment in Swiss watchmaking was cut, in three years between 1979 and 1982, from 65,000 to 15,000.

And, while the high value of the Swiss franc and a world recession had something to do with the loss, the main antagonist was that quartz watch.

As Michel Mamie, director of the European Watch and Jewelry Fair, said in a *Christian Science Monitor* interview in 1982, "The electronic watch needs no special knowledge. Anyone can make it...it can be produced very simply."

He went on to explain that the Swiss watchmakers thought the change would occur very slowly. They had predicted that electronic watches would have only 15 percent of the market by the year 2000. Now they account for almost 100 percent of cheaper watch production.

But let us get back to the question, Who invented it? The correct answer to the question is

the Swiss!

In 1967, the Swiss watch manufacturers' research arm, The Swiss Watch Federation Research Center at Neuchatel, created the first prototype.

They presented it to the Swiss manufacturers, and, while there is no public record of the response, we can guess at some of the comments:

"It doesn't tick!"

"It looks too clumsy!"

"What do you mean, it has no gears? No springs? No jewelled bearings? How can it even be considered a watch?

And, some nastier things were probably said, too. But the end result was that the manufacturers turned their research group into "outsiders" and rejected the idea. Let me quote from *Fortune* magazine, January 14, 1980, to capture what really happened.

> ...The main villain proved to be the inflexibility of Swiss watchmakers. They simply refused to adjust to one of the biggest technological changes in the history of timekeeping, the development of an electronic watch...Swiss companies were so tied to traditional technology that they couldn't – or wouldn't – see the opportunities offered by the electronic revolution. It was a classic case of vested interests blocking innovation.

Vested interest sounds too much like selfish, purposeful, contriving. I contend that their old paradigm simply blocked them from being able to even begin to see the new one. It is a story worth remembering.

In-a-Rut Warfare

Technology, science, culture, personal experience, simple experiments, games – you can see the influence of paradigms in all of them. Paradigms have direct and indirect influence on the ways of the world. Perhaps one of the most dramatic examples of the paradigm effect occurred after World War I with the French. World War I was basically trench warfare. After that war was over, the French decided to protect themselves **forever** from the Germans by constructing a great linear fortress. They set to work on one of the largest engineering projects in the history of humankind: the Maginot Line.

The Maginot Line was the culmination of the trench-warfare paradigm. It was made up of underground forts, underground tunnels, underground railways, virtual underground cities—all connected in a line between France and Germany. It was the final answer!

Of course, we know what happened. Germany chose not to fight with the old rules. Instead, they created the new paradigm—*Blitzkrieg.* The Germans surprised the Allied armies by attacking through the Ardennes with a massive mobile armored force. They simply outflanked the Maginot Line. And, with the collapse and demoralization of the French army only weeks after this maneuver, the Germans were able to cross with impunity the impregnable Maginot Line. All because of a paradigm shift.

Japanese Management, Again

This example is one that I always save until last because it has caused so much discussion in the last decade.

Let me start by asking you to respond to the following question: In 1962, what were the kinds of judgmental or qualitative terms that you would have used to describe any product with the following three words stamped on it:

MADE IN JAPAN

Please fill out your list below.

1. _____

2. _____

3. _____

4. _____

5. _____

Now compare your list to the list I've been collecting for the last several years:

Junk	Trivial
Poor Quality	Cheap
Unreliable	Low Tech
Tacky	Tin Cans
Second Rate	Plastic
Shoddy	Crummy
Worst Choice!	Second Choice
Poor Copy	Third Choice
Toys	Imitation
Unimportant	Lousy

Well, you get the idea. Now, let's ask another question. Please fill out in the space provided below the descriptive words that you would have used in connection with these three words today:

MADE IN JAPAN

1. _____

2. _____

3. _____

4. _____

5. _____

Now, let's compare your list to the list I've been collecting:

High Quality	State of the Art
Highly Reliable	Best in the World
Fine Quality	First Rate
Excellent	Zero Defects
Inexpensive	World Leader
Copy	First Choice
Sophisticated	Innovative
Best Buy	High Tech

If you'll notice, the two lists are filled with antonyms. Because of that, we should look at **what happened** in Japan between 1960 and 1980 to create such a dramatic turn of events? Of course, many of you know the answer, but I want to put it into my context.

They changed their manufacturing paradigm.

It actually began in the early '50s when W. Edwards

Deming, an American, was invited by General Douglas McArthur to come to Japan to present his ideas on high-quality mass production. He so impressed the Japanese that they ultimately created a prize called the Deming Award. It is the most honored of all industrial awards in Japan.

Deming gave them a powerful quality-control-and-improvement paradigm. The Japanese then blended in the work of Professor Kaoru Ishikawa of Tokyo University to create the quality-circle paradigm, a simple concept whose major premise was that workers on the line probably will have the best ideas for improving the product. On top of that, there were other management innovations and cultural traditions already in place that allowed the Japanese to begin to build a new way of management and manufacturing.

So, by the late '60s and early '70s, products began to appear from Japan in American stores and automobile showrooms that were impressive in their quality and durability.

American management responded to these anomalies by finding logical explanations, the classic response from the prevailing paradigm community.

Initially, American manufacturers explained it this way: "Well, they have new factories, we have old factories, so, of course, their products should be better than ours. If we had new factories, we could do just as well."

That seemed a good explanation until a series of studies were made comparing the products coming out of factories of equal ages. Then, surprise! Even with same-age factories, the Japanese products were better.

So American management offered a second explanation. "It's Japanese culture. They have a homogeneous culture; their workers are well educated; they speak the same language; they have the same values; they have corporate unions; and, most of their workers are from the rural areas. So, of course, they would be able to produce better products because the communications and agreement would be so much easier than in America where we have a heterogeneous population with multiple languages, sophisticated union leaders, and a whole range of educational backgrounds."

The explanation was generally accepted until the mid-'70s when Sony Corporation built a TV factory in San Diego, California, one of the most heterogeneous of all cities in America–Anglos, Blacks, Hispanics; multiple languages, including "Californian." Yet, despite all this diversity, within three years, Sony named the San Diego plant as one of their top ten plants in the world. All of a sudden, American management was left with no explanations, except one: The Japanese management system was superior to ours. They were producing high-quality products not because of a factory advantage or a cultural advantage but because of a management advantage. And, since 1977, when American business finally understood what was going on, we have been running at a frenzied pace to catch up to the Japanese by attempting to learn and implement their management techniques.

I can think of no more powerful example than the Japanese-management paradigm to show you what can happen when a paradigm changes. I would submit to you that the Japanese-management paradigm has created an **epidemic of quality** throughout the world. And any organization that doesn't catch this disease may have a very difficult time surviving the next twenty years. The Japanese have brought high quality to mass production and demonstrated how everyone can afford the best because best is no longer a function of price. I believe that, in the 21st century, one of the most important paradigm shifts from the 20th century will be the Japanese model of how to produce high-quality, low-cost, zero-defect products.

From these nine examples, I hope you can see how broad the spectrum of paradigm influence is. From the physiological level, which is the most dramatic kind of influence, to the simple but still important judgment level, where something is perceived as impossible to do and is therefore ignored.

To ignore the power of paradigms to influence your judgment is to put yourself at significant risk when exploring the future.

8   *Key Characteristics of Paradigms*

While I could go on and on with examples, now it is time to draw some conclusions about paradigms based on the examples in this book. There are seven characteristics which are important for everyone, but particularly so if you are concerned with innovation or want to be an entrepreneur.

1) Paradigms are common

Thomas Kuhn didn't believe this. In his book, he concludes by saying that only in the fields of science can we have paradigms and paradigm shifts, because only scientists are precise enough and careful enough to write things down and follow the rules. He suggests that even some sciences, such as the social sciences, are in their "preparadigmatic" time. In spite of his assertion, I think, and many others agree, that paradigms abound in the real world. They can be found in all phases of life from science, where we have over-arching paradigms such as quantum physics and recombinant DNA biology, through political paradigms, through paradigms of art and music and food and dress, to organizational and corporate paradigms, to professional paradigms of the engineer, the lawyer, the doctor, the brick layer, the futurist; to such simple paradigms of everyday life as politeness and cleanliness. These deserve the label paradigms because each activity is bounded by rules and regulations that discipline and direct behavior, including problem solving, and that set standards which must be met in order to be considered part of a community. Without question, there are rules to all of these "games."

You'll find that there are paradigms all around. Many are trivial; that is, the rules and regulations do not impact on the larger environment much, if at all. But they have the same effect as more important ones by giving the practitioner special vision and understanding and specific problem-solving methods.

2) Paradigms are functional

You may have concluded because of the many comments I have made about the effects of paradigms and their influence that I see paradigms as something undesirable, but I don't. In fact, I don't know how human beings would get along without them. They are necessary. We need rules to help us live in this highly complex world. Without rules for direction, we would be constantly confused because the world is too rich with data.

Paradigms are functional because they help us distinguish information which is important from that which is not. The rules tell us how to look at the information and then how to deal with it.

Let me share an anecdote from my family life to illustrate this utility. My son, Andrew, watched me play tennis for many years, but, until he was fifteen, he wasn't interested in the game. Then he took some lessons. After he began playing, he said to me one day in passing, "I'm going to enjoy watching the U.S. Open with you this year." I asked him why. He said, "Now I know what to look for." Andy was learning the tennis paradigm. Before he took his lessons, when he had looked at tennis on the TV screen, he saw two people in white clothes running all over a green area hitting a fuzzy little white ball back and forth between them. But because he had no point of reference, no rules by which to under-stand and evaluate what they were doing, it was meaningless.

As he learned to play the game, he learned the rules of tennis. He understood a drop shot, a top-spin forehand, a slice backhand, a half volley, an overhead. He understood the concepts of strategy, and, all of a sudden, what was meaningless data for him before on the TV screen became understand-able, interesting, and useful, as a direct result of learning a paradigm. We all experience that new understanding when we learn a paradigm.

3) The paradigm effect reverses the common sense relationship between seeing and believing

Remember the cliché, "I'll believe it when I see it!" From what I have been describing in this book, I would suggest that the reverse is more accurate: "I'll see it when I believe it." In other words, subtle vision is preceded by an understanding of the rules. To see well, we need paradigms. As a teacher, I saw it happen in my classes. When I was explaining something to my students, many were unable to understand it even though the information was directly in front of them. But, as they began to understand the principles, the rules, the paradigm, they would say, one by one, "Oh, now I get it." What they were getting were the rules; what they were gaining was a subtle change in vision.

This third point is especially important for people who are employers. It explains why some new employees have a difficult time of adjustment. What they are really doing is adjusting to the paradigms of the organization, and, until they know those rules, they will literally be unable to see things that are obvious to people who have been there for a while. The temptation is to think these people not intelligent enough to handle the job. The fact is, they may have more than enough intelligence; they simply lack the understanding of the particular paradigm.

The other side of this situation offers a special opportunity to an employer if he or she is willing to take advantage of it. Those who don't know the rules lack the ability to see things the way trained employees see them. On the other hand, they still have the ability to see things that are important, that can no longer be seen by those who have learned the organizational paradigms. With their fresh vision, new employees are very much like the paradigm shifter described in chapter four. They don't know what should and shouldn't be done, they don't know what can and cannot be done, so they may see a way of doing something that is better than what is presently being done.

For that reason, I strongly recommend that all new employees have an interview after their first thirty days in which their supervisor asks a simple question: "What do you see around here that surprises you, that you think is unusual and could be improved?" And, then, the supervisor should just sit back and listen. More often than not, he or she will be rewarded.

So, new employees respond to both sides of the "seeing and believing" characteristic of paradigms. Treat them gently until they learn to see. Use their naive perceptions to your advantage to see yourselves anew.

4) There is almost always more that one right answer

In his book, *Ascent of Man,* Jacob Bronowski writes about the impossibility of identifying the right answer: "There is no absolute knowledge, and those who claim it – whether they are scientists or dogmatists – open the door to tragedy. All information is imperfect. We have to treat it with humility." (p.353)

The effects of paradigms explain why this must be the case. By changing my paradigm, I change my perception of the world. This does not have to mean I must have contradictory perceptions, just that I am seeing another portion of the world which exists equally as well as the portion that I saw with the other rules. But because one paradigm allows me access to one set of information and another paradigm allows me access to another set, I may end up with two different, yet equally correct, explanations of what is happening in the world.

All you have to do is look at the number of right answers researchers have developed in the last decade for the world energy problem, and you can see how true this is. Anyone who assumes there is only one right answer is missing the point of the importance of paradigms.

5) Paradigms too strongly held can lead to Paradigm Paralysis, a terminal disease of certainty

Paradigm paralysis is, unfortunately, an easy disease to get and is often fatal. More than a few organizations, which were dominant in their prime, succumbed and died of it. It is like "hardening of the categories." It grows from a situation of power. We all have our paradigms, but, when one is successful and in power, there is a temptation to take our paradigm and convert it into **the** paradigm. After all, isn't it what made us successful? Once we have **the** paradigm in place, then any suggested alternative has to be wrong. "That's not the way we do things around here." This problem can occur at all levels and will, in the long run, throttle new ideas.

In non-turbulent times, absolute positions may not be immediately dysfunctional because change occurs more slowly. One set of rules may last a long time. But, in turbulent times, to have **the** right way to do things and no ability to explore alternatives is extremely dangerous. What was right six months ago could become wrong because of a major, rapid change in the environment.

Arthur C. Clarke writes in *Profiles of the Future*, a book first published in 1962 and recently reissued, "It is really quite amazing by what margins competent but conservative scientists and engineers can miss the mark when they start with the preconceived idea that what they are investigating is impossible." (p. 21)

He said it another way, too, which is now stated as Clarke's First Law, "When a distinguished but elderly scientist states that something is possible, he is almost certainly right. When he states that something is impossible, he is very probably wrong." (p. 29)

This characteristic of paradigm paralysis has implications for innovation. Why is it that internal innovation is so difficult to stimulate? Because **the** paradigm is already in place. So, until we can change that attitude and stimulate people to be more flexible and break out of their paradigm paralysis to search for alternatives, we will continue to find the great new ideas, on the whole, being discovered outside the prevailing institutions.

6) Paradigm Pliancy is the best strategy in turbulent times

Paradigm pliancy is the opposite of paradigm paralysis. Paradigm pliancy is the purposeful seeking out of new ways of doing things. It is an active behavior in which you challenge your paradigms on a regular basis by asking the Paradigm Shift Question:

What do I believe is impossible to do in my field, but, if it could be done, would fundamentally change my business?

I asked that question to a supercomputer company's senior management team in the early '80s. They knew the answer – parallel processing. Parallel processing is done by hooking up many small computers to run in parallel. Doing so would speed up the ability to compute while lowering costs by as much as 90 percent. But no one could do it.

Today you can buy parallel processing computers. By the mid-'90s parallel processing computers will dominate many segments of the supercomputer market. To recognize that impossibility a decade before it happened gave my clients time to prepare. And they did.

Another question useful to ask is:

Who, outside my field, might be interested in my unsolved problems?

These two questions will help you begin the search for your new paradigms, and by actively searching you greatly increase the likelihood of finding them.

Here's a good first step toward paradigm pliancy. When someone goes **against** your paradigm, fight your natural tendency to explain why it is impossible and, instead, say:

"I never thought about it that way before, tell me more."

And, then, be quiet and listen. You'll be surprised at how many good ideas you will hear.

7) Human beings can choose to change their paradigms

It is this observation about paradigms that makes me such an optimist about the future. Human beings are not genetically encoded with only one way of looking at the world. In fact, our coding seems to give us the capability to look at the world in a wide variety of ways.

If you are religious this ability to change is called Free Will. If you are not, it's called self-determination. The result is the same—you can choose to see the world anew.

What happened with the environmental movement is a perfect example of this ability to change. If you had done a survey of businessmen in the early '60s about the correctness of the emerging environmental paradigm, most of them would have said it was a bunch of B.S. – crazy radicals spouting crazy ideas. Twenty years later, most business people not only agree with the environmental observations, they can articulate, at least as well as those '60s radicals, why the rules are important. "Yes, it **is** important to have clean air, Yes, it **is** important to have clean water. Yes, it **is** important to take care of waste disposal...because it's bad business if we don't." In fact, it is turning out to be good business to take care of the environment.

By the way, there is a corollary to observation 7: Since I've run into the paradigm concept, I've discovered that there are very few irrational people in the world. When I am talking to someone who has a severe disagreement with my observations, I am on the alert for a disagreement not of fact but of paradigms. Almost always that is the explanation for the disagreement. The person is looking at the same things I'm looking at but using a different set of filters to examine the information; and, as a result, they see different things.

Kuhn suggested that you must consider, when talking to a person with a different paradigm, that you are talking to a person with a different language. Until you can speak their language, you will not be able to communicate clearly. I think that is excellent advice.

So, when I get into a disagreement, I've learned to quiet down and listen. Almost always the person will sooner or later tell what his or her paradigm is, and, once I understand it, I can begin to understand what he or she is saying. I may still disagree, but at least I know why.

By understanding these seven aspects of paradigms, I think you can improve your understanding of what influences your perceptions and be more open to new ideas.

9

The Evolution
of Paradigms

It is time to return to the graphic description of paradigm development that I noted in chapter three.

After reading about and researching paradigm shifts for five years, I began to work on a way of graphing the development of new paradigms; I called this the evolution of primitive paradigms. What I was looking for was a way of explaining to my audiences the pattern of development that a paradigm goes through.

First, let's refresh our memories about the parts of the pattern (figure 3): the horizontal axis is T for Time; the vertical axis is PS for Problems Solved. When I say Problems Solved, I am talking about new problems solved, not just solving the same problem repeatedly. That means that each mark on the vertical axis indicates a new problem solved with the application of the paradigm; the form of the curve is the classic S shape.

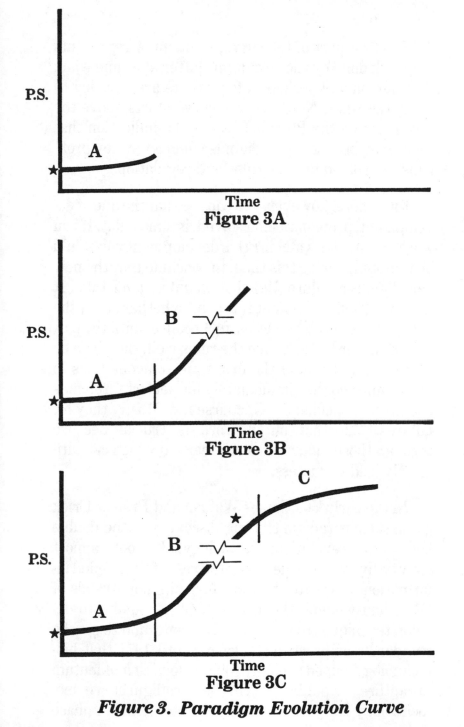

Figure 3A

Figure 3B

Figure 3C

Figure 3. Paradigm Evolution Curve

The first part of the curve, segment A represents the work done by the paradigm shifter at a time when that person and perhaps a few others are learning to apply the rules. Note that the curve starts above the zero point on the PS axis because the indication that there may be a new paradigm is when a few key problems are solved by new rules and regulations.

From here, however, you can see that the line of development, problems being solved, is almost flat. If you were an outsider watching this development you would be tempted, during this time, to conclude that the new paradigm is a failure. But that would be a mistake. It is very difficult to know at this point whether or not the new paradigm will be successful because, until the paradigm shifter learns to use the rules well, there can be no real test. Think of the first time someone tries to play tennis: do they immediately hit perfect forehands and perfect backhands? Of course not. Mostly they hit failures. But that initial work is crucial because through those failures much is learned which can ultimately lead to success.

In the early '50s, James Watson and Francis Crick made their paradigm shifting discovery of the double helix that revolutionized biology. It took almost twenty-five years to decipher the rest of the needed information, to create the tools for snipping strands of DNA and welding them back together again, to develop techniques to read the DNA code, and to set the standards for practice. It wasn't until 1977 that biotechnology gained enough problem-solving momentum to capture the public eye. On the paradigm curve, biotechnology has just barely moved out of the A phase into the B phase. Ten years from now, we will look back at this time as the Wilbur and Orville Wright era of biotechnology.

The Women's Movement is also early into the B phase of its development. This epochal shift has to break so many old male-dominated paradigms that perhaps three generation from now, the world will see some substantial change. But right now, there are only a few nations who are seriously committed to the shift, and many who seriously oppose it.

Once the rules are understood and the users have some facility with them, the shape of the curve changes. The inflection of the curve represents three important changes in the use of the paradigm:

1) An improved ability to apply the rules;

2) A clearer understanding of the boundaries, of exactly what to apply the paradigm to;

3) The arrival of the pioneers who bring brain power and enthusiasm to the new paradigm.

Segment B of the curve is a dynamic time because, since nobody has applied these rules to these problems before, the new practitioners are very successful. What has happened in biology during the last twenty years is a perfect example. You can trace its development through the initial sputterings of the paradigm. For instance, it took a Harvard team more than a year to decode the first very simple DNA strand. Now we have computerized machines that do it automatically.

So, up the curve we move, with our support technology improving, our sophistication improving, our brightest people now joining because they see the new paradigm as a hot new area of opportunity.

The upward length of this curve is determined, I believe, by the generalizability of the paradigm. The more profound the paradigm, the more new problems it can solve, the longer the curve upward. The mark of a great paradigm is its ability to continue to climb that curve. But, sooner or later, the development gets to the C phase.

The C phase of the curve represents two aspects of change in the paradigm's evolution. First, it is beginning to run out of the problem set. It has been applied to many of the problems it is appropriate for. Second, it is dealing with all those very sophisticated problems that were not worked on earlier because they were very tricky or they needed special technology. Because of the cost and sophistication of these problems, it takes more time, more money, and more people to solve them. But this added time and cost put the paradigm under pressure to "pay back" those expenses. So, as the speed of problem solving slows down and the costs begin to climb, there is a growing concern by the paradigm community.

The C phase is a crucial time for a paradigm because the pressure begins to mount to be more efficient. Yet, that is not to say the problems being worked on are not important. It is just that it looks like the paradigm has run its course. And this appearance increases the likelihood that young, bright people are going to look for another way to deal with the remaining problems because they don't want to get trapped in a dead end. So, the C phase represents the old age of a paradigm, and during this time people who had previously been very critical of alternative paradigm development become more open to changing their paradigm.

There are two other curves that also may be useful in describing the pattern of paradigm development. These curves represent only mental models, but when I have shared these concepts with some of my audiences, they have been intrigued by them. Both measures are provocative.

First, **Problem Solving Efficiency** (figure 4): The Y axis becomes Problem Solving Efficiency (PSE). I believe that paradigms can be measured for their efficiency by dividing the number of problem solutions attempted into the number of problems actually solved. As this number gets closer to 1.0, the more efficient the paradigm.

A paradigm begins very inefficiently, which is logical because the practitioners are not yet skilled at using it. Then the paradigm begins to grow much more efficient as the skills improve. The tapering back is not the result of loss of skills but rather the increasing difficulty of the remaining problems; and problems are still being solved. But the efficiency measure does decrease.

When I have asked my audiences if they could place their own paradigms on this curve, many of them felt they could. Their placement, for the most part, was

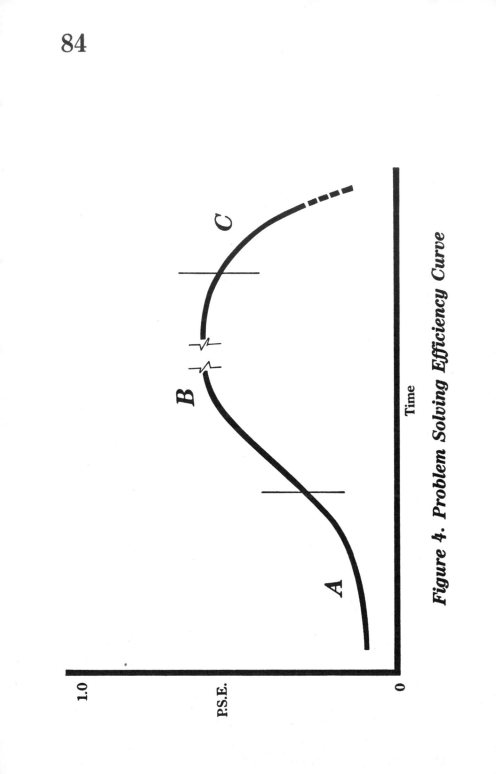

Figure 4. Problem Solving Efficiency Curve

marked by the "feeling" of efficiency because no one had, immediately at hand, data that would demonstrate the efficiency measure.

Now let's change the Y axis again. This time it will represent **Cost Per Problem Solved** – CPPS (figure 5). It starts off quite high. That is because it may take one person several months or even several years to solve the first problems. The long time frame is a result of the lack of understanding and practice with the new paradigm so a lot of mistakes and wrong turns are made.

The turn-down in the CPPS is driven by getting a better understanding of the use of the rules. And as the cost drops, more problems can be solved with the given resources so the paradigm continues to evolve rapidly.

It is worth mentioning here, again, that each "problem" is a new problem. In profit-making situations, there is a lot of money to be made solving one problem repeatedly, and, in some cases, these single solutions can make so much money for an organization that they do not have to care very much about the CPPS. In the case of nonprofit organizations, a single important problem solved can create so much good will that the CPPS will be ignored for some time.

When the curve turns upward, it is usually to address those "great" problems which have been waiting for the sophisticated paradigm practitioner or the funds necessary to underwrite the necessary technological support to do the work. In 1985 the European physics community proposed the construction of a 60-mile-in-circumference, $4 billion particle accelerator so

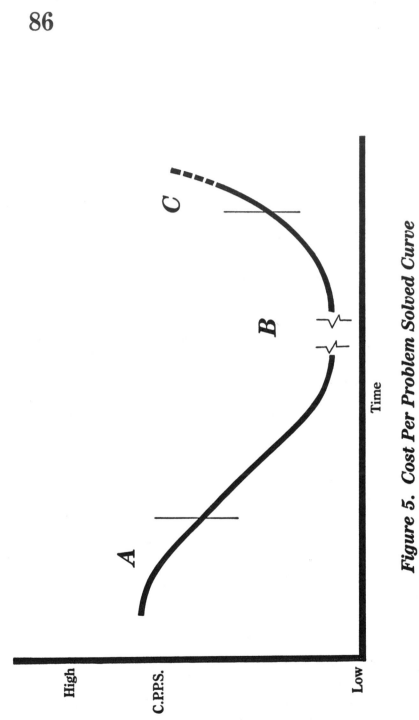

Figure 5. Cost Per Problem Solved Curve

they could investigate some of the most difficult questions in physics. That is a perfect example of high cost per problem solved! While the growing cost factor may seem like a death knell, it is not necessarily so in business-for-profit paradigms. If the problems solved yield large profits, a company can afford to continue. But, even if it can afford to continue, this rising cost situation will catalyze others who are not enjoying those profits and who want to get in the business to look for other ways, less expensive ways, to solve the problems. This search is, for all intents and purposes, a search for a new paradigm.

When the cost per problem solved becomes too high (and cost can be defined in either-or-both time and money), the paradigm is ready to be challenged.

Yet, even when the indicators grow more negative, many of the prevailing paradigm practitioners respond in an obtuse way. Since they are so deeply invested in their present paradigm they are very likely to continue to ride the negative side of the curve rather than to look for a new paradigm.

The reason for this behavior is simple. As long as they are still solving some new problems, they see themselves as successful; they are still maintaining their status, and they do not have to relinquish the power which they gained by being part of the present paradigm. However, as fewer new problems are solved, and more go unsolved, someone somewhere will try to develop a different set of rules and regulations to deal with those unsolved problems.

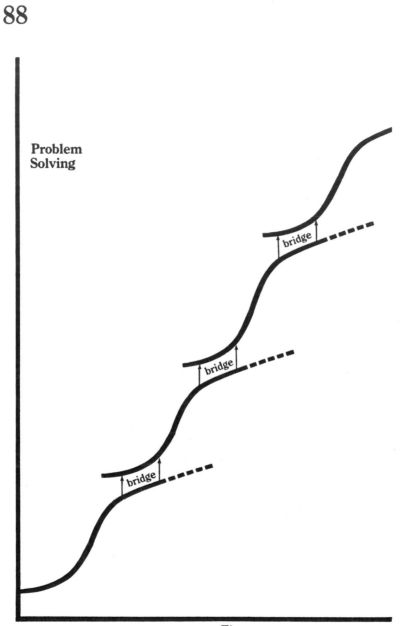

Figure 6. ***Paradigm Bridging***

Choosing to ride the wrong side of the efficiency and cost curves guarantees that the practitioners will end up in a massive crisis. They are heading for disaster. When they finally realize that a disaster is about to happen a dramatic change in behavior occurs – they become remarkably paradigm pliant! The reason for this about-face is simple: **they have no choice**. It is change or die. Even the most recalcitrant will usually change given that choice. Look at the Japanese response to Dr. Deming. They really had no choice but to listen to him. He probably would have been ignored before World War II. But in 1952 they were desperate.

But, remember, choosing to change at the bottom of the efficiency curve is the **worst position** from which to shift paradigms. Far better to begin to change your paradigm while you are still high on the curve and have money and time. By waiting until you are in crisis, you greatly reduce your likelihood of success and you probably will get only one chance to make a change.

The ideal pattern of shifting paradigms looks like figure 6. Always begin the search for the new rules while the old rules are still successful. Then you maximize your leverage from the old paradigm to bridge to the new paradigm and give yourself time to prepare for the shift.

10 *Going Back to Zero*

There is one more observation about the effects of paradigm shifts worth discussing. This last observation helps explain why entrepreneurs can be so amazingly successful and how a special kind of equality between established, powerful organizations and new endeavors is created with the emergence of new paradigms.

When a new paradigm appears, everyone goes back to zero.

By zero, I mean that whatever leverage one had because of the old paradigm is dramatically diminished with the emergence of the new. This gives the creator of the new paradigm a very special chance to compete with established titans of the old paradigm. This is not immediately obvious from just talking about the curve, so let me illustrate.

One of the most powerful examples of the back-to-zero effect can be found with the development and marketing of the personal computer. If I had written in 1975 that two young men, neither of whom had finished his college education, would create in their garage a computer that would force the IBM Corporation (which then held more than 60 percent of the world computer market) to drastically change, within five years, its methods of manufacturing, software production, sales, and machine security, how many of you would have taken me seriously?

But that's exactly what happened. Steven Jobs and Steve Wozniak did it when they created their Apple computer and its marketing strategy. Their rules were simple, brilliantly so.

When the Apple II came out in 1977, there is no question that people at IBM and other mainframe computer companies laughed. And, yet, by 1982, almost all of them were trying to emulate Apple's paradigm.

Now, let's check my "everybody goes to zero" thesis by setting down four rules that IBM was following in 1975 and which were very important in their wonderful success.

1) IBM manufactured the heart of their computers, the microprocessor, themselves. In fact, they were one of the best at that in the world.

2) IBM always wrote the software for their computers using their own very talented software groups.

3) Without fail, IBM products were sold by IBM super sales people, the best in the world at what they do.

4) No one was allowed to open up an IBM product except an IBM person. In some cases to remove the cover of an IBM product voided the warranty.

Now, IBM had other rules, too, but in the '70s these four were clearly part of a successful IBM paradigm.

Then along came Apple. Jobs and Wozniak wanted to get into the computer business, the personal computer business. And to do that, they created a new approach, a new model, a new paradigm. Let's take a look at their rules:

1) Since Apple couldn't afford to manufacture their own microprocessors for their little computers, they bought them from a vendor – an outside source.

2) Since Apple couldn't afford to hire a lot of software people to write programs, they hired a software house – an outsider – to help them write software.

3) Since they were a brand new company and had only minimal sales people, they sold their products through retailers in stores across the country.

4) To encourage broader use of their product, they designed the Apple to be opened by the users (in

fact, they fastened the top with pop-open fasteners to make taking off the top easier) and put in empty card slots to invite the user to add new products from Apple and other manufacturers that would enhance the power and flexibility of their little computer.

Please note the dramatic difference between the IBM rules and Apple's rules. Then note how IBM finally got into the personal computer market in 1982:

1) IBM did not manufacture the PC's microprocessor. Instead, they bought it from a vendor (just like Apple did).

2) IBM got key parts of their PC software written by a vendor just like Apple did. (Microsoft, to be exact, the same software house that helped Apple!).

3) IBM sold their PC through retailers like Sears, Computerland, and others (exactly the same way as Apple).

4) And, just like Apple, IBM made it easy to get inside their box and put in empty slots for others' equipment.

And Apple did it all first! Even mighty IBM who had their own powerful and successful computer paradigm had to switch to Apple's rules in order to play the new game. And the effects are not finished yet. In order to get into the game IBM created a special independent business unit and its success has spurred other groups in IBM to ask for the same structure so they could bring out new products. Jobs and Wozniak have had quite an effect on one of the world's greatest companies simply by creating their new paradigm.

At this point, however, I should point out one more company rule that IBM did not violate. That rule is: IBM always gets their fair share of the market. And, in order not to break that rule, they broke the other four.

By the way, I am not being critical of IBM. On the contrary, I applaud their ability to step outside their own highly successful paradigm and adopt another paradigm in order to compete in this market. Someone at the top understood that when the rules change, they had to change, too. They could not play the PC game with old IBM rules; they had to play the game with Apple rules. Obviously, they will now begin to try to mutate the Apple rules to use more and more of their inherent leverage based on the IBM paradigm. It will be interesting to watch that process.

Here is the key point in this discussion: Apple wrote the rules. They were a good set of rules that added up to a powerful new paradigm. The result was that others followed. With their rules, Apple defined a market that did not exist in 1975. Within ten years, it will be a $20 billion market because of a new paradigm.

This, then, is the leverage of changing paradigms. If you are the paradigm shifter **and** you have the stamina to get through segment A into segment B on the evolution curve, you have enormous leverage. If you are a big company, and this new paradigm challenges your old paradigm, you cannot assume that you will automatically have special leverage from your old paradigm.

A final thought on going back to zero. When IBM joined the PC paradigm, they forced the problem-solving curve almost straight up. Literally thousands of programmers and hardware designers began solving problems only because IBM joined the game. The numbers of new software packages coming into the market every month because of IBM's presence demonstrates the drawing power of those three letters – IBM.

By straightening up the curve like that, IBM made it very difficult for others to get into the game. Where there had been a one- to two-year window of opportunity before IBM, IBM closed it to a matter of months. So, to play the game, many decided to copy IBM's product hoping that IBM underestimated the market. And that is exactly what happened. One company, Compaq, became a $100 million corporation in one year by producing an IBM perform-alike that was transportable. But this strategy of copying leaves the copier very much at the mercy of IBM.

There is an alternate strategy which another company took to deal with the power of IBM's presence. "Change the paradigm or a significant portion of the paradigm." And the company who did that was, surprise!, Apple. That is exactly what they tried to do when they introduced Macintosh (Lisa, an earlier computer, was an attempt which failed. It did not have the right combination of rules to successfully challenge the

IBM PC). The Mac has many aspects that are radically different from the IBM PC: small, easy to use, a "mouse" to control the computer actions, a printer that literally reproduces whatever is on the screen, a 32-bit microprocessor. These differences represented a significant enhancement and moved Apple substantially higher on the curve. So, while a lot of people laughed at the little Mac when it was introduced, it now is perceived as a canny move on the part of Apple.

In a very real sense Apple said to IBM, "Now that you're so good at our old game, we're improving the game." It is going to be fun over the next decade to watch the give and take between these two companies.

To be able to identify primitive paradigms significantly improves your ability to anticipate the future. By spotting them early, you can then track and monitor them. At some point, you will have to choose whether or not to accept that they are no longer a crazy idea but the beginning of a new way of doing things. The sooner you can identify them, the more likely you will be able to take advantage of the potential leverage inherent in an emerging paradigm and the more you can protect yourself from the damage that the new paradigm will create as it supplants and overrides the old paradigm.

11

Looking Forward

I have spent most of this book talking about the concept and process of paradigm change and have used historical illustrations to make my points. But this isn't a book about understanding the past; it is about exploring and anticipating the future. So the logical question at this point is: can we apply the paradigm concept to discover the potential shifts between now and the year 2000? Since I am a process futurist, my emphasis has dominantly been on how to think about that question, but at this point it is both relevant and appropriate for me to switch gears and play content futurist.

Let me start by suggesting a verbal test for paradigm shifts. If we talk about "more" of something or "less" of something in the next fifteen years, we are **not** talking about paradigm shifts. Those are trends, and, as I said before, while they are important to identify, we want to identify the more powerful elements for change–paradigm shifts. So, here is the test. It captures the essence of paradigm change.

First we think of a new approach, a change that we believe might be a paradigm shift. Then we ask ourselves how we would respond to the old, 1985 approach in comparison. Using this "look back" mode from the vantage point of the year 2000, we should find ourselves responding with incredulity–

"Did we really do 'it' that way back in 1985?"

If there is surprise at the great contrast between the 1985 approach and the new approach, then we probably have identified a paradigm shift.

If that seems like too simple a test, try it by going back twenty years and you will see that it works surprisingly well. For instance:

Did we really believe it should be "The buyer beware"?

Did we really think high school and college sports were just for the boys?

Did we really think nuclear power was the ultimate answer for producing electricity?

Did we really think we could dump all those toxins into the water and not have horrible consequences?

Did we really think good automobiles had to

weigh 5000 pounds and only had to get ten miles to the gallon?

Did we really think that Blacks (remember when Whites called them Negroes?) were happy as they were?

Did we really believe all women were supposed to get married, have children, and stay at home?

Did we really think short hair on men was the only "manly" way to look?

Did we really think outer-space research was a waste of time and money?

Since 1982, whenever I have had enough time with my audiences, I have asked them to identify some paradigm shifts that they think may occur by the year 2000. With some groups I have let them be as general as they wished. With other groups I asked them to be specific to their own industry or profession. In late 1984, a delightful group of nurse administrators from the state of Illinois generated the following list of potential paradigm shifts in health care. This list represents only the first twelve items of a much longer list. Take a look at it and see if you agree with their observations.

Potential Paradigm Shifts
in the Health Care Field 1985-2000

1) Patient diagnosis will occur at home.

2) The consumer will drive the health-care system rather than the other way around.

3) Babies being born at home will be the norm.

4) More jobs will be available in our field than people to fill them.

5) Nurses will be independent contractors rather than employees.

6) Medical care will be rationed.

7) The male/female ratio of nurses will be equal.

8) Large hospitals will have disappeared.

9) No invasive surgery will be done.

10) Donation of organs will be mandatory.

11) Measurements of the quality of life will be as important as the quantity of life.

12) Genetic engineering on the preborn will be common.

This is just one example list from one group. And look at the dramatic predictions! Look at the contradictions (i.e., 9 and 10). I am sure every professional group, every industry, can write its own list of potential paradigm shifts.

Now it's your turn. Before you read my list, take a couple of minutes and write down the paradigm shifts you see, first for your own field of interest, then for the larger society. If you can't think of a specific shift but you feel there is an area where a paradigm shift is really needed, then list the area. Just acknowledging that there is a potential for such a change is an important step to becoming more aware of forces that may cause that change to occur. The paradigm shifts that are described after this section will be societal changes only.

Paradigm Shifts of Personal Importance for Me

1. _____

2. _____

3. _____

4. _____

5. _____

Potential Societal Paradigm Shifts

1. _____

2. _____

3. _____

4. _____

5. _____

With the paradigm test in mind, I would like to share with you the ten most common changes listed by my audiences in the last three years. I have added comments where I thought they would be worthwhile. Remember that these audiences have been very diverse but the majority are business groups of middle and senior managers.

Space Industrialization

It is obvious to anyone who understands what a paradigm shift is that the industrialization of space represents a fundamental change in the way we choose to produce things. Already we are working on the production of drugs manufactured on board the space shuttle. When we get a permanent space station with proper production facilities, materials literally impossible to produce on the surface of the planet become easy to make. Just one example may be foamed metals. On earth it is impossible to foam metal because the weight of the metal collapses the bubble before the metal hardens. But in outer space where only microgravity exists, the process can be done. Foamed metals have extaordinary properties, among them being high strength with extremely light weight. Also, since they would be refined in an almost perfect vacuum and in a containerless environment, these metals would be purer than anything ever produced on earth.

What revolutions this one product from outer space could have on our planet boggles the imagination. What kinds of bridges could we build, or buildings could we erect? Think of the low weight, supersafe, high mileage automobiles that could be fabricated from foam metals. Or airplanes? The new paradigm of zero-gravity manufacturing in outer space has not even begun to be understood, much less explored.

The Electronic Cottage

Alvin Toffler covered this paradigm shift thoroughly in his book, *The Third Wave*, but it is worth a quick review here. The electronic cottage is a direct result of the explosion of personal-computer (PC) use. The idea is simple: since I can work on my PC anywhere, why not do some or much or all of my work right out of my home instead of driving into the city to go to the office to do my work. Hence, the electronic cottage.

By letting people stay at home to work, two problems of contemporary society can be mitigated – child care and elderly care. Instead of institutionalizing the kids and the grandparents, an adult can be around to help them and work with them. On top of that advantage, the electronic cottage also welcomes into the workforce people who cannot leave their homes because of illness or a handicap. It also reduces energy use by reducing car use. It increases the safety of neighborhoods by having more adults around. And recent studies have demonstrated that those working alone in the home environment find their productivity increasing by as much as 50 percent.

All of these reasons help support this radical repositioning of the workforce and constitutes a fundamental change in our present employment paradigm.

Universal Communication

Phones without wires. A simple trend extrapolation? Most of my audiences believe phones without wires constitute a paradigm shift not a trend extension because without wires, and using satellites to connect the phones, impossible dreams become reality.

First of all, there will be no such thing as long distance. Or to put it another way there is no such thing as short distance because every call must go up 22,500 miles and come back down that same distance. On a scale like that, it is irrelevant in terms of cost and time delay as to whether that signal starts in St. Paul, Minnesota and comes down in Bombay or in Minneapolis. So, one price covers all calls.

Second, the ability to find someone anywhere in the world (as long as they don't turn their phone off) becomes an easy problem to solve. Simply by triangulation, a specific signal could be located to within meters of where that person is.

Third, the costs to institute such a system in third-world countries is far less than the cost of putting in wired phone systems. In other words, universal communications through satellite networks is the cheapest way to give everyone a phone. Talk about "reach out and touch someone!"

And lastly, in our security-conscious United States, if a person felt they were in danger, they could turn on their phone and put out a signal that would alert the police to their need and their location. Even as they were running from a potential attacker, their ongoing signal would let the police find them.

This wireless system also carries with it a privacy loss that will have to be dealt with. Unless some kind of signal scrambling is done, anyone with the right equipment could listen to your conversation. But, in one sense that is no worse than today. Still, it is a significant downside to this paradigm shift which may retard its development until satisfactory solutions are found.

Solar Energy

No group that I have spoken to has left this item off the list. They all want some new rules in energy and I think the fact that solar energy is consistently brought up represents a special perception on the part of my audiences. Can we have solar energy **at a significant level** by the year 2000? Not if you listen to what Exxon tells eveyone in their EPCOT energy show at Disneyworld in Orlando.

But things are happening in spite of Exxon's pessimistic predictions. The Japanese have taken an American invention, amorphous silicon cells, and have figured out how to mass produce them. And, in early 1985, ARCO, an American oil company, announced a breakthrough which would, they claim, make solar cells competitive with oil by 1990! Wind farms, using a specific form of solar energy, are beginning to become cost competitive with expensive energy sources such as oil and nuclear power. The challenge lies in committing to the effort in a way equivalent to our commitment to energy conservation in the '70s which dramatically changed the energy-use rules in America. If my audiences are right, fission nuclear power has no support. Solar energy is the next step.

Robotics

When I am working with manufacturing groups, robotics is almost always one of the first three paradigm shifts listed. For other groups it comes later. The robots that the manufacturing experts think about bear little resemblance to the science fiction robots. Unlike R2D2, most robots in the world today are stationary units with one arm. They do repetitive work very well. Assembly of small elements, painting cars, fitting doors in mobile home manufacture, and jobs such as that are their specialty. Their strength is their reliability, their precision, and their exact costs. Unlike workers who can get sick, go on strike, or hurt themselves on the job, robots are very predictable, very controllable.

In fact, this is a confused area as yet because the exact perception of what a robot really is does not exist. The confusion exists because some robotics experts suggest that robots are basically "steel-collar" workers instead of blue-collar workers. I think they are missing a fundamental difference that defines one of the keys to this paradigm shift. Robots are not workers but **slaves!** Please note the definition of a slave: "a bond servant divested of all freedom and personal rights; a human being who is owned by and wholly subject to the will of another, as by capture, purchase, or birth." We need only strike the words "human" and "birth" and we have a workable definition of our robots.

Dealing with slaves is quite another thing than dealing with workers. Workers have rights; workers have expectations; workers, as fellow humans, need to be part of decisions and interactions and can make important contributions as participatory management techniques have so vividly demonstrated. But slaves? They must be taken care of, yes, so they can maintain their productivity. But other than proper maintenance, they may be used exactly as needed. Period.

Robots are getting smarter and more talented by the month. Skills such as pattern recognition, vision, touch are coming out of the laboratories and into prototypes with amazing speed. As their talents increase, so will the new robotics paradigm have to be adjusted and refined to deal with them. They will not only fundamentally change the manufacturing process, (i.e., one line of robots producing many different products on demand, rather than specialty lines that can produce only one product and must wait unused until there is demand for that specific product), but robots also dramatically intrude into the economics of the world.

A simple, disturbing, and as yet unanswered question: "Who gets the wealth that the robots generate?" If it is the stockholders of the company, then who buys what the robots make? Certainly not the displaced workers who have no jobs. All the displaced workers can't be retrained to fix robots and program robots because those jobs will likely be displaced by the robots themselves. And, as we improve the design and quality control of robots, we will have less fixing to do. Ultimately, of course, the robots will assemble themselves, and maybe even design themselves. When that happens, we will have another paradigm shift to deal with.

There is a very disturbing cycle apparent in this

paradigm shift that no one I know has addressed successfully. I think we had better spend some time thinking about how to deal with the implications of this new paradigm before we get too far along into the change. Without some careful exploration of the future of robotics, we could be creating the climate for extreme turbulence.

This example illustrates how paradigm shifts that look technologically positive can be socially very negative unless they are thoughtfully introduced and implemented.

Electronic Shopping

"Gee, did we really drive to shopping centers to do all of our shopping back in 1985?" A surprisingly large number of people believe that by 2000, the shopping-center paradigm will be dramatically changed. All those four-color catalogs we receive in the mail each month are considered to be a precursor to this change in the way we buy things. But the new shopping paradigm is very different, indeed, when you look closely at what is happening. Buying out of a catalog is still driven strongly by emotion and influence of "pretty pictures."

The next step is the addition of our personal computer to help us shop in an electronic marketplace. When the personal computer is factored in, then the buying mode becomes something altogether new. With your PC, you will be able to instruct it to do your shopping. You simply give it the criteria you want the product to fulfill, and it goes searching in the electronic marketplace to find it. For instance, you want to make a major purchase of a car. So you list your criteria in order of importance:

1) Must get seventy-five miles per gallon (this is year 2000 remember);

2) Must have four doors;

3) Must be very quiet on the road at 100 mph;

4) Must seat five in comfort;

5) Must cost less than $20,000.

6) Must be available at a car dealer within five miles of dwelling.

There may be other criteria but you get the point. With those instructions, your computer begins to search through the data bases on automobiles and, at the end of the day, when you have finished your work, you call up its answers. Listed for you in prioritized fashion will be the cars that fulfill your criteria. You now have excellent information from which you can make an informed consumer decision. Also, you have avoided the emotional aspects of shopping for that car. That does not suggest that emotions are no longer a part of the decision – you still may decide based on the most beautiful of the cars that fill your criteria. Or you may find that none of the cars that do fill your criteria is acceptable. But with electronic shopping you dramatically improve your ability to make those decisions objectively and quickly. There is an interesting tangent worth taking here.

Think of the impact of PC shopping on advertising. So much of it now is designed **not** to inform you of the real characteristics of the product. How must it change to deal with a truly informed consumer who will have the rational information for decision-making before he or she even begins to take a hard look at which product to buy? Will the advertisers try to convince the consumer not to use the computer as a shopping helper? Or will a new age of truth and clear information come about to minimize the impact of PC shopping? If I were an advertising agency, I would be thinking very hard about this paradigm shift.

Wellness

As you may recall from chapter ten, I stated that when a field has a very high cost-per-problem-solved ratio, it makes itself a candidate for a paradigm shift. Present day medicine, sometimes inaccurately labelled "health care," is one of those candidates. In 1984 it constituted 10.8 percent of the gross national product. If its cost trend continues, it will be 25 percent of the gross national product by the year 2000.

Most of my audiences see a new paradigm to replace the old. It is called **Wellness**, and several of my client companies have already instituted wellness programs to reduce their corporate health care costs.

Wellness is based on a simple assumption: if we really practiced being healthy, we wouldn't get sick as severely or as often. This concept flies in the face of traditional medicine that doesn't waste its time with you until you've got something to cure and basically is done with you as soon as you are "not sick." But not sick is only halfway toward being extremely well. It is this positive area that wellness resides in.

In the early '70s, a group of paradigm shifters began exploring a very important question, "What's better than Not Sick?" They began by talking to people who exhibited dramatic "Not Sick" behavior; in other words, High Vitality/Well behavior. The interviewers discovered that many of these well people shared a set of common traits:

1) They got regular and vigorous exercise in which they breathed a lot of clean air. In other words, they got aerobic exercise.

2) They ate moderately, and their diet had much more complex carbohydrates (fruits and vegetables), much less fat, and a broader mix of protein sources (less red meat, more chicken, fish, and vegetable protein) than the standard American diet.

3) They demonstrated the ability to deal with emotions on a very broad spectrum; from deep sadness all the way up to extreme happiness. "Well" men, for instance, had the capacity to cry easily over emotional situations. While they managed stress well, clearly they did much more than just that. They also had strong relationships with other people.

When people with these practices were measured for their "illness quotient," they were found to be sick very little, if at all. They had a much lower incidence of heart disease, cancer, ulcers. In other words, they were very healthy people.

Armed with their studies, advocates of wellness went to the doctors and hospitals to talk about a new kind of health-care system. But the response of the illness-care providers to wellness was classic paradigm paralysis. Most doctors simply said it wasn't their business. Most hospitals looked upon it as a fad and ignored it.

But now, in the '80s, Wellness is almost out of the A section of the paradigm development curve. The question is: will the doctors and hospitals be too late to become a major force in the new approach to medical care?

Banking

A change in the banking paradigm has been mandated by the deregulation of the industry. It is axiomatic that deregulation forces a change in paradigms because it is the withdrawal of the old rules.

The dilemma for the practitioners of the old paradigm is that they are not given a new set of rules but instead are left to create the new rules. Of course, because there are no new rules, anyone else who wants to get into the game can come and help write the rules.

And this is exactly what has happened. Right now three of the major players in the financial industry game could not have played in the old game. They are

Merrill Lynch–a stock brokerage firm, Shearson/ American Express–a credit card company, and, of all people, Sears–a department store/catalog company!

While many banks have watched somewhat befuddled, these three companies plus several other outsiders have moved into the territory and are working hard to create the new paradigm of financial management. American Express has purchased the IDS Corporation, an old-line mutual-fund company with great connections in middle America. And Sears bought a real-estate company, Coldwell Banker.

What is clear as this book is printed, is that there is no agreement yet on the next banking paradigm, and so the search continues. What is also clear is that outsiders who never before could have played the game are serious contenders for the future of this extremely important sector of the American and world economy.

Bio-Manufacturing

This topic makes the top ten in the paradigm shift list under several headings–biotech, recombinant DNA manipulation, genetic engineering. What it amounts to is using the new biological paradigm based on the coding system for living things, DNA, to manufacture products organically. Regardless of the title, it represents a dramatic change in rules.

Every week there is some kind of announcement about a breakthrough in biotechnology. This explosion of problem-solving indicates that biotech is out of its A stage of development and into the B stage.

So dramatic are some of the breakthroughs that they would have been considered miracles twenty years ago. And we have only begun with this new paradigm. One particular example I know of is an outstanding indicator of where we are heading in this field.

Dr. James McAlear is a biophysicist and entrepreneur who is trying to use biotechnology to "grow" a computer. Yes, grow a computer! While that sounds crazy, Dr. McAlear is convinced it can be done. He has received grants from such significant organizations as the U.S. Navy to underwrite his work. Using biotechnology to manipulate DNA, he is attempting to produce organic integrated circuits. And once he gets one such circuit, the rest of his computer should follow. This carbon-based approach to computers would revolutionize the computer industry because **mass production would become re-production** and lower the cost of producing even giant mainframe computers to levels where anybody could afford one.

This new production approach, growing what you need instead of assembling it, is actually the ultimate return to where we started. Except now we are controlling the process rather than merely being a result of the process.

Education

Education is last on the list of the paradigm shifts, though it is certainly not the least of the ten. In many ways it is the most important. Today's education system has all the attributes of a paradigm that is finished in its present form. The defense it receives by its practitioners represents its last gasps. In 1983 the National Education Association explained to the American public that all it needed to correct the poor education given our children was more money for the teachers. More money has never resurrected a dying paradigm; it merely prolongs the agony.

Education in its present form is being challenged by the parents, the corporations who are hiring its products, and by the students themselves who know they are getting a bad deal. The calls for change are at a fundamental level not at a cosmetic level.

There are three elements which may trigger change in the present educational paradigm.

1) **Home computers.** One of the measures of parental concern about education is the number of computers that are being purchased to be used in the home as an educational aid. Initially educators ignored this trend but now it has become significant. Perhaps the most significant aspect of this change is that the educational programming being purchased for the home is not selected by the teachers, but by the parents for their children. This represents curriculum control taken out of the school district's grasp. Without that power exclusively in their control, teachers lose their leverage to direct exactly what students must learn. This represents a fundamental change in

the decision-making about what topics students ought to study and which authors they ought to read.

2) **Vouchers.** Vouchers are checks provided by the state and federal governments that can be used to buy education. Instead of this money flowing directly to school districts, state and federal governments would send vouchers to the parents of school children. The parents then can give the voucher to whichever school they wish to. This represents a powerful lever in the hands of parents because the school district receives the money only if the parents decide to send their children to that school. If they want to give the voucher to a private school and make up the difference with their own money they can do so. If they want to give it to a parochial school they can do it. It puts the public school into the educational marketplace and forces the public school to be more responsive to parental concerns. And, perhaps most importantly, it underlines the fact that students are the clients who must be treated well, not just persons who must, whether the teacher performs well or not, sit through the class.

3) **National Testing of Students and Teachers.** Already the teacher testing has begun and has been met with great resistance from teacher organizations. They explain that to expect tests to demonstrate the "important" aspects of a teacher's skills is ridiculous. Of course, parents have to

wonder about the tests the teachers give which ultimately measure the skills which will or will not get their children into prestigious colleges and universities. Why do the teachers' tests of students have validity but the tests of teachers lack it? While the resistance to teacher testing will continue, another effort, national testing of students at all levels, may end up testing the teachers through their students' performances. What is becoming clear is that teachers need "quality circle" help from their students to become better teachers. Without clear feedback from their clients, teachers will have a difficult time of discovering where and how to improve.

After saying all that, it is still very unclear what the new paradigm will look like. Enough to say, that the three forces mentioned will have a big impact on forcing change. The pushing has begun toward meeting the need. I wouldn't be surprised, at all, if the new educational paradigm comes from the corporations of America instead of the educational institutions. Present educational institutions have the potential to be one of the huge growth areas of the United States in the 21st century. But they must change dramatically to gain that role.

While these ten potential paradigm shifts are important for all of us, they are by no means the only ones that may happen. It would be easy to extend the list to twenty or thirty or forty. The point of this exercise is to demonstrate that many people in all walks of life believe and expect fundamental change in the next twenty years.

Even if we are wrong about 75 percent of these changes, the remaining 25 percent is more than enough to change the nature of the way we live. Your challenge then, is to learn to discover these new futures soon enough to prepare for them.

12

And So It Goes

"No matter how much you study the future, it will always surprise you; but you needn't be dumbfounded!" *Kenneth Boulding*

I was at a lecture in 1975 when Dr. Boulding, a professor of economics, said that, and I thought how perfectly it explains why we spend time trying to explore the future. There will **always** be unanticipated events. That is the nature of the universe. But there are many events which are discoverable if one takes the time to look for them. And the search for those protects us from "dumbfoundedness." That is why the concept of paradigms is so useful.

I have made the following points in this book about paradigms:

1) Our perceptions of the world are strongly influenced by paradigms.

2) Because we get so good at using our present paradigms, we resist changing them.

3) It is the outsider who usually creates the new paradigms.

4) Practitioners of the old paradigm who choose to change to the new paradigm early must do so as an act of faith rather than as the result of factual proof, because there will never be enough proof to be convincing in the early stages.

5) Those who change to a successful new paradigm gain new vision and new approaches for solving problems as a result of the shift to the new rules.

6) A new paradigm puts everyone back to zero, so practitioners of the old paradigm, who may have had great advantage, lose much or all of their leverage.

As a conclusion to these observations, I have suggested that, in turbulent times, it is to your best advantage to develop and actively practice paradigm pliancy.

In *Ascent of Man*, Jacob Bronowski speaks to pliancy in his chapter, "Knowledge or Certainty." He focuses on the Heinsenberg Principle of Uncertainty and suggests it should be renamed the "Principle of Tolerance" which ". . . fixed once and for all the realisation that all knowledge is limited. It is the irony of history that at the very time when this was being worked out by physicists there should rise, under Hitler in Germany and other tyrants elsewhere, a counter-conception: a principle of monstrous certainty." (p. 367)

The Hitlers of the world demonstrate the worst kind of paradigm paralysis and what can happen when a person in power persuades others to join him in that belief. But the condition of despotic certainty can be found to a lesser degree in experts who choose to tell the rest of us why certain things are impossible.

For instance, the great film maker, D. W. Griffith, said in the early 1920s, "Speaking movies are impossible. When a century has passed, all thought of our so-called speaking movies will have been abandoned. It will never be possible to synchronize the voice with the picture."

Another expert in transportation was quoted in *Literary Digest* of 1889, "The ordinary 'horseless carriage' is a luxury for the wealthy; it will never, of course, come into as common use as the bicycle."

Scientific American, 1891, offered the following observation about the Panama Canal; that it "...is a thing of the past, and Nature in her works will soon obliterate all traces of French energy and money expended on the Isthmus."

And the idea of flying always received bad treatment. Simon Newcomb, an astronomer of some note, said in 1902, "Flight by machines heavier than air is unpractical and insignificant, if not utterly impossible."

These were only a few of the erroneous predictions pulled together for *Quest Magazine* of January/February 1981 by Jane and Michael Stern. They make the point in an historic way about the dangers of certainty.

At the very least, the certaintists end up looking like fools; at the worst, they block the serious examination of important but radical ideas.

In his book *Profiles of the Future*, Arthur C. Clarke builds two lists that exemplify this discussion. One list is of those inventions expected during the 20th century and the other is the list of discoveries or inventions no one ever mentioned:

The Expected – Telephones, automobiles, flying machines, steam engines, submarines, robots, death rays, transmutation, artificial life, immortality, invisibility, teleportation

The Unexpected – X-rays, nuclear energy, radio, TV, electronics, quantum mechanics, relativity, transistors, masers & lasers, super-conductors, atomic clocks, determining the composition of celestial bodies, neutrinos, dating the past with Carbon 14, detecting invisible planets, the ionosphere, van Allen belts, pulsars

Clarke composed these two lists in 1962, so there are other elements that could be added to the unexpected list that would make it even more dramatic. The point of the second list is simple: perfect anticipation cannot be expected. And, on top of that, one major unanticipated paradigm shift creates ripples of other changes that can make the future significantly different from an otherwise logical forecast without that major change incorporated.

All the more reason for an open attitude. An attitude of tolerance and openness keeps available the huge potential of **conceptual leverage,** that springs from new ideas that can change the world, the very paradigm shifts that I have spent this book writing about.

Now it is time to acknowledge explicitly that which has been implicit in all that I have written. You probably have come to the conclusion that I have been offering for your consideration

a paradigm of paradigms

I have been giving you a set of rules for understanding and manipulating paradigms. I have suggested the boundaries of this paradigm; I have suggested the problem-solving capability of this set of rules; I have offered antecdotes/models of how this paradigm works; and I have suggested to you that by using this conceptual framework you can dramatically improve your ability to explore the future.

What does this mean to you at this point? First, there is an **act of faith** that you will have to go through if you are going to use this paradigm. I have not given you enough proof to make you certain. And, second, only if you go out and try these rules for observing the world will you find out if I have given you something worthwhile. Only if you start solving problems that you couldn't solve before, explaining behaviors that you couldn't explain before, seeing the world in a new light and with new vision, will you become convinced of this paradigm's worth.

I have tried to offer you clear directives so you can

become a better strategic explorer. I have based those directives on the paradigm concept.

Now the testing is up to you. I said at the outset that your single most important skill as a strategic explorer is to understand how your vision is shaped, what influences your perception. Without that understanding, all the other skills will be only minimally useful.

Now, let us reflect back on Drucker's comments about turbulent times: **Significant competitive advantage lies with those organizations and individuals who anticipate well in turbulent times.**

What I have been suggesting throughout this book is that much of the turbulence of our times is caused by: 1) the failures of old paradigms (and the attempts to prop up those outmoded rules) and, 2) the creation and introduction of new paradigms.

While trends have made the headlines for the last couple of years, these are not the chief causes of turbulence. Trends are much easier to perceive because they have history, they leave a path from which we can forecast their direction. Because trends have clear direction, instead of causing turbulence, they actually help reduce it because they have a significant amount of predictability. Even if we do not like the shape and content of the emerging trends, they at least give information that allows us to anticipate certain consequences. Of course, explosive trends can cause great turbulence; but most trends take time to gather momentum, and we can use that time to reduce their negative impacts on us and optimize the opportunities they hold for us.

Imbedded in the paradigm discussion is a special kind of feedback loop for innovation which James Bright, one of the pioneers of technology forecasting, has been examining. One of the observations Bright makes about innovation is that it is spurred on by turbulence, or "crisis," as he calls it. In times of crisis (high turbulence), people expect, in fact, **demand**, great change. This willingness to accept great change generates two results:

1) More people, responding to the demand for great change, put in time trying to find new ways, i.e., new paradigms that will resolve the crisis, thus increasing the likelihood of paradigm shifts.

2) More people are willing, because of the crisis mentality, to accept fundamentally new approaches to solve the crisis, thus increasing the opportunity to change paradigms.

And this sets the stage for radical change. Let me give you the following sequence to think about:

Step 1: The established paradigm begins to be less effective;

Step 2: The affected community senses the situation, begins to lose trust in the old rules;

Step 3: Turbulence grows as trust is reduced (the sense of crisis increases in Bright's terms);

Step 4: Creators or identifiers of the new paradigm step forward to offer their solutions (please note that many of these solutions may have been around for decades waiting for this chance);

Step 5: Turbulence increases even more as paradigm conflict becomes apparent;

Step 6: Affected community is extremely upset and demands clear solutions;

Step 7: One of the suggested new paradigms demonstrates ability to solve a small set of significant problems that the old paradigm could not;

Step 8: Some of the affected community accepts the new paradigm as an act of faith;

Step 9: With stronger support and funding, the new paradigm gains momentum;

Step 10: Turbulence begins to wane as the new paradigm starts solving the problems and the affected community has a new way to deal with the world which seems successful.

At this point, with the affected community increasingly comfortable with the new paradigm, the level of tolerance for more new ideas drops dramatically, and the cycle is complete. Now we must wait for the next round of significant problems that the newly accepted paradigm cannot solve to trigger a new cycle.

Obviously, during turbulent times, many more paradigms are going to be proposed than accepted.

Many are unsuccessful paradigms. Others are marginally acceptable. A few will become the prevailing paradigms. Our challenge as strategic explorers, whether our role is that of manager, politician, educator, or citizen, is to make it easier for the new paradigms to get a fair hearing and to help the paradigm shifters feel safer.

It is still a great risk in our society to offer new rules for the game.

One of my corporate clients responded to exactly this point and created a program which I think is exemplary. The specific division I was working with was known for its unwillingness to think radically, so the woman in charge of improving their attitude toward innovation created a "Trial Balloon" Day. On those days, about once per quarter, people could sign up and meet at an off-site location with an evaluation committee. The committee, schooled in the concept of paradigms and their influence, would listen to the new idea and examine its merits and risks with the innovator. If it was a good idea, the committee, plus the innovator, would carry it up to the next level. If the idea was inappropriate, the innovator could leave anonymously—no embarrassment or funny stories and jokes behind his/her back. The response to the Trial Balloon Day has been very positive, because it reduces the risk of suggesting new paradigms.

It is that kind of willingness that we need throughout our society during these turbulent times. Because only if we are willing to looking broadly at new ideas and new ways of solving problems, will we find the caliber of innovation that we will need to move into the 21st century successfully. The society that innovates the best will most probably lead the world for the first generation of the new millenium.

The Last Chapter

In this book I have tried to indicate the power and influence of paradigms, to explain why we cling to our old paradigms, to suggest some reasons for being more open to new paradigms. I have stated that, during turbulent times, we need to actively search for and anticipate the future.

Now it is your turn to do some work. If you accept what I have been saying, then I would like you to do the following things:

Take an inventory of your present paradigms by writing down what you believe to be the "right" way of doing things or acting in the following areas:

• Your job—especially the management style, (i.e., I believe in breaking deadlines rather than releasing shoddy products. When the product is excellent, and not before, is when it will be released.)

• Your family life (i.e., close physical contact with my kids is a necessity for helping them grow up healthy.)

• Your morals (i.e., lying always creates more problems than it solves.)

• Your politics (i.e., a country without affordable legal protection for everyone cannot be a just country.)

• Your religion (i.e., do unto others as you would have them do unto you.)

• Your view of the rest of the world (i.e., most Asian cultures have a much stronger sense of the importance of a long-range vision of the future than Western culture. They are willing to think 200 years ahead and plan for it.)

Look for rules/beliefs that focus your attention and create the base by which you measure others. Any time you have a "Thou shalt not..." you have part of a paradigm.

If you are married, you might ask your spouse to do the same thing. Comparing notes can be an insightful activity. By the way, one of the best tests of what your rules are is what you teach your children. You may break some of your own rules, but usually what you try to teach your children is what you hold others up to for judgment.

In addition to the above, there are two more exercises I would like you to do:

Write a list of rules which other people practice but which you disagree with. This list will help identify areas of paradigm conflict for you.

Now ask yourself, what conditions would force you to alter your present paradigms? For instance, you may be against stealing, but, under certain conditions, you may find yourself willing to steal. This examination is very important because it allow you to explore conditions under which you would alter your present paradigms.

After you have listed the paradigms by which you direct your life, you can begin to monitor how they help you solve problems and how they get in the way of solving other problems. Once you are aware of your rules, you can look for changes in the world which may impact on your paradigms and challenge them. Or you can choose to start changing them for reasons of your own.

Remember what I said earlier: I am not against having paradigms; they help us deal much more effectively and efficiently with life. But I believe we need to keep flexing them and testing them in these turbulent times.

One more recommendation for those of you who want to do something with this concept: The cheapest, most powerful way to stretch your paradigms and improve your strategic exploration skills is to read. I read sixty publications per month (including four dailies), because it is my business to stay in touch with new ideas. I offer you a more modest goal. Below is a list of seven books to read and then nine publications to monitor (in order of priority).

The Books:

The Structure of Scientific Revolutions, Thomas S. Kuhn, (University of Chicago Press, 1962)

Limits to Growth, Dennis Meadows et al. (Signet, 1972)

The Aquarian Conspiracy, Marilyn Ferguson, (Tarcher, 1980)

An Incomplete Guide to the Future, Willis W. Harman, (Norton, 1979)

Small is Beautiful, E. F. Schumacher, (Harper and Row, 1972)

The Third Wave, Alvin Toffler, (Morrow, 1980)

The Eighth Day of Creation, H.F. Judson, (Simon and Schuster, 1979)

Each of these books presents a dramatic alternative to some of today's paradigms and will challenge many of your paradigms as they did mine. Check your response to their ideas. Find your boundaries. Consider theirs. You can't help but stretch.

The Publications:

The Christian Science Monitor, a daily, 1-800-456-2220. If I could choose only one publication to monitor future possibilities, this is it. Not only does it cover emerging technologies and social issues well, but it has a global perspective. No other publication even comes close to CSM in terms of its breadth and depth of exploration of important issues of the future.

Science News, a weekly, 1-800-247-2160. This little publication is usually only twelve pages long, and summarizes brilliantly the new scientific and technological information of the past seven days. It is written for the lay person and has one major feature each time. The best bargain in science information.

The Atlantic Monthly, 1-800-525-0643. For technological types, this is your balancing publication. It regularly covers social/political issues of great future importance.

Mother Earth News, a bimonthly, P.O. Box 70, Hendersonville, NC 28739. Doing things differently is the mark of this publication. It is pro-environment, pro-small business, pro-self-reliance. It reflects the ideals and paradigms of a special minority in the United States and regularly describes important alternative ways to solve significant problems.

Popular Science, a monthly, Time Mirror Magazine, Inc., 380 Madison Avenue, New York, NY 10017. This publication has expanded its perspective in the past ten years and now reports not just "Gee Whiz" technology but a broad range of technologies. Its strength is that it is usually first to publish wild new inventions and innovations. It takes the time to illustrate and describe these concepts so that you can get a good idea of their possible applications.

Wall Street Journal, a daily, 11 Cortlandt, New York, NY 10007. Too bad they don't publish a monthly summary of their great stories. Their Op Ed page has great columns often suggesting major business paradigm shifts and, at least once a month, a front-page story gives insight into changes in the business world that you should be aware of.

The Futurist, a bimonthly, World Future Society Headquarters, 4916 St. Elmo Avenue, Bethesda MD 20814-5089. This is the official publication of the World Futures Society. While it could be stronger editorially, the concepts explored every other month are worth your time, if for no other reason than to see what the professionals are writing about. It regularly focuses on social/political innovations and their implications.

Technology Review, a bimonthly, 1-617-253-8292. While the above publications cover much of the emerging technological ideas, *Technology Review*, published by M.I.T., offers special insight because of the way it focuses with such depth on single issues. I have always found at least one important thought in every issue I've received.

Brain Mind Bulletin, a twice monthly, 1-818-577-7233. This nifty little four-page newsletter is the result of the efforts of *Aquarian Conspiracy*'s author, Marilyn Ferguson. Beautifully summarized, the information is always at the edge of the brain-mind paradigm.

It is clear from my list that my biases are toward the sciences. That is because right now they exert so much influence on everything we do. Since science and technology are driving forces right now, it is only logical that we keep careful watch.

Final Thoughts

We live in the time of paradigm shifts. Not everyone can formulate successful new paradigms. Only a few do that. But all of us can be more open to looking for the changes, exploring them for their implications, and creating a supporting climate for the attempts. There is no question that, in many areas, we need new paradigms. In ever increasing frequency, the call for innovation goes out across the United States, and around the globe. Paradigm shifts are one of the key innovative behaviors.

Question: who is scouting the future for us? Answer: lots of people. What I mean is this: one person's paradigm shift may be another person's reality. Somewhere in the world, alternative paradigms are already part of a system. The United States is scouting the future of communications; England is scouting the future of family computers; Japan has been scouting the future of participatory management; the Soviet Union is scouting the future of information repression. Just by looking around the world, we can find many other paradigms that may allow us to solve significant problems of our own.

Let me conclude this book by offering four quotes and one story.

> **It is important**
> **not to mistake**
> **the edge of the rut**
> **for the horizon.**
> *Anonymous*

> **Those who say it cannot be done**
> **should get out of the way**
> **of those who are doing it!**
> *Anonymous*

> **The real act of discovery**
> **consists not in finding new lands**
> **but in seeing with new eyes.**
> *Marcel Proust*

> **No corporation gets hit**
> **by the future**
> **between the eyes,**
> **they always get it**
> **in the temple!**
> *Dick Davis*

This last quote is my favorite, because it's true for all of us, not just corporations. Looking forward only in one direction leads to a special kind of strategic blindness. One must scan the horizon constantly to identify the important changes occuring on the sidelines, at the edges. After all, isn't that what exploring is all about?

A Final Story: The Pig and the Sow

Once upon a time, there was a man who had a cabin in the mountains and a Porsche to get there. Every Saturday morning, he would drive up to his cabin on a very dangerous road filled with blind curves, unguarded dropoffs, and tricky turns.

But this man was not bothered by the danger. After all, he had a great car to drive, he was an excellent driver, and he knew the road like the back of his hand.

One fine Saturday morning, he was driving to his cabin. He was coming up to one of his favorite blind curves. He slowed down, shifted gears, and put on the brakes in preparation for the turn which was about 200 yards away. All of a sudden, from around that curve, came a car careening almost out of control! The car nearly went off the cliff but, at the last second, its driver pulled the car back onto the road. The car swerved into his lane, then back into its lane, then back into his lane again.

My God, he thought, I am going to be hit! So he slowed almost to a stop.

The car came roaring on toward him, swerving back and forth. Just before it was about to hit him – at the last moment – it swung back into its lane. As it went past him, a beautiful woman stuck her head out the window of the car and yelled at him at the top of her lungs, "PIG!!"

What?! He thought, How dare she call me that! He was incensed by her accusation! Instantly he yelled after her, "SOW!!!" as she continued down the road.

"I was in my lane! She was the one who was all over the place!" he muttered to himself. Then he began to get control of his rage; he smiled and was pleased that at least she didn't get away without his stinging retort. He'd gotten her good, he thought smugly.

And with that, he put the accelerator to the floor, raced around that blind curve...**and ran into the pig!**

That is a paradigm story. You see, he thought the woman was calling him a name. But she was really doing a heroic thing. In spite of the fact that she had almost been killed, she took the time to try to warn him about the pig on the road around the curve. But he had paradigm paralysis. He thought she called him a name; so he followed "the rules" and called her a name...and thought that was the end of it.

Actually, he had demonstrated the beginnings of some flexibility when he noticed that it was she, not he, who was swerving all over the road. If he had had paradigm pliancy, he would have responded to her shout by asking himself, **What is going on?** Then he would have driven around the corner much more cautiously. At the least, he would not have hit the pig. At the most, he could have stopped, picked the pig up, put it in his trunk, and driven away with it.

The moral: during the next decade many people will be coming around blind curves yelling things at you. They will be too busy to stop and explain, so it will be up to you to figure it out.

If you have paradigm paralysis, you will be hearing nothing but threats.

If you have paradigm pliancy, you will be hearing nothing but opportunity!

I would submit, in the context of all that I have said, that the choice of which you hear is entirely up to you.

Thank you for reading my book.

Additional Paradigm Tools

Books

Additional books may be ordered through Charthouse Learning Corporation. The cost is $17.50 plus shipping. Call for information about quantity discounts.

Their toll free number is (800) 328-3789.
In metro Minneapolis/St. Paul call (612) 890-1800.

Or you may write to:
  Charthouse Learning Corporation
  221 River Ridge Circle
  Burnsville, MN 55337

Discovering the Future – the film

DISCOVERING THE FUTURE, the film/video-tape has rapidly become a best-seller in the business world. Over 3,000 organizations world-wide are using this program to help encourage innovation and deal more successfully with change. The film deals with many of the key concepts in this book, and can effectively communicate the paradigm message quickly throughout your organization.

A comprehensive 80-page facilitator's guide including exercises, a complete transcript, and master visuals is also available.

"It amazes me – the single viewing of a film can so dramatically affect the way I think!"
    – John Welshons, Winston-Seabury Press

"The response has been phenomenal."
    – Thomas Rowlett, IBM

"This film has literally turned our people around in a willingness to look for radical solutions to problems. This is, by far, our most requested program."
    – Ted Miller, Merck, Sharp & Dohme

For information on rental, purchase, or preview of this program, contact Charthouse Learning Corporation

Their toll free number is (800) 328-3789.
In metro Minneapolis/St. Paul call (612) 890-1800.

142

Or you may write to:
Charthouse Learning Corporation
221 River Ridge Circle
Burnsville, MN 55337

Profiting from Paradigms — an audiotape series

PROFITING FROM PARADIGMS is a collection of 6 audiotapes that contain over two and a half hours of comprehensive paradigm exploration. Joel Barker shares his latest stories and examples of the paradigm concept in action. This is perhaps the most complete discussion yet by Joel Barker, and it contains many field- and industry-specific recommendations.

The tape set costs $120.00, and is available through Charthouse Learning Corporation.

Their toll free number is (800) 328-3789.
In metro Minneapolis/St. Paul call (612) 890-1800.

Or you may write to:
Charthouse Learning Corporation
221 River Ridge Circle
Burnsville, MN 55337